- Mary, Mary   67
- One, two, buckle my shoe   68
- Little Jack Horner   69
- Hot cross buns   70
- Jack Sprat   71
- Old Mother Hubbard   72
- Three blind mice   74
- Simple Simon   75
- Curly Locks, Curly Locks   76
- One, two, three, four, five   77
- Ding, dong, bell   78
- Jack and Jill   79
- Little Bo-Peep   80
- Little boy blue   81
- Tom, Tom, the piper's son   82
- There was a crooked man   83
- There was an old woman   84
- As I was going to St Ives   85
- Ladybird, ladybird   86
- The north wind doth blow   87
- Little Tommy Tucker   88
- Goosey, goosey, gander   89
- Wee Willie Winkie   90
- The man in the moon   92
- Hey, diddle, diddle   93
- Ride a cock-horse   94
- Ride away   96
- Here comes a lady   97
- A farmer went trotting   98
- This is the way the ladies ride   99

- Father and M   00
- To market, to   01
- Rocking-horse   102
- Trot, trot, trot   103
- Dance, little baby   104
- Katie Beardie   105
- Dance to your daddy   106
- Down at the station   107
- Higgledy-piggledy   108
- Rub-a-dub-dub   109
- Cock-crow   110
- Handy-Spandy   111
- Barber, barber   112
- Clap, clap handies   113
- Diddle, diddle dumpling   114
- Doggie's way   115
- Up to the heavens   116
- See-saw Sacradown   117
- The little duck   118
- Hob, shoe, hob   119
- Three little ghosties'es   120
- Shoe a little horse   121
- Bye baby bunting   122
- Sleepy song   123
- Lullaby   124
- Baby beds   125
- Evening   126
- Notes on interactive rhymes   127

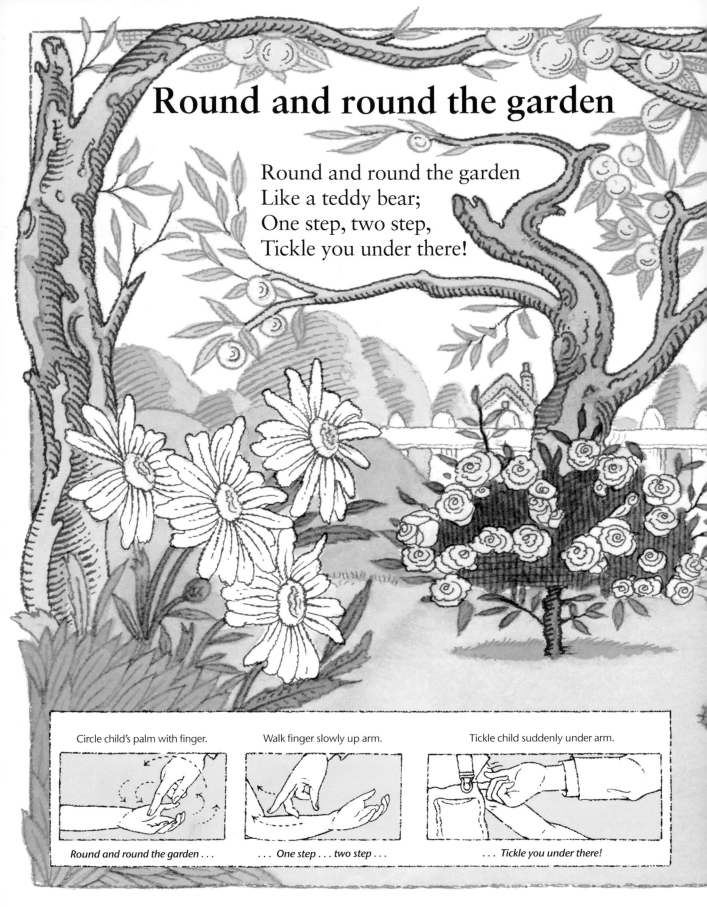

Round and round the garden

Round and round the garden
Like a teddy bear;
One step, two step,
Tickle you under there!

Circle child's palm with finger.

Walk finger slowly up arm.

Tickle child suddenly under arm.

Round and round the garden . . .

. . . One step . . . two step . . .

. . . Tickle you under there!

Five fat sausages

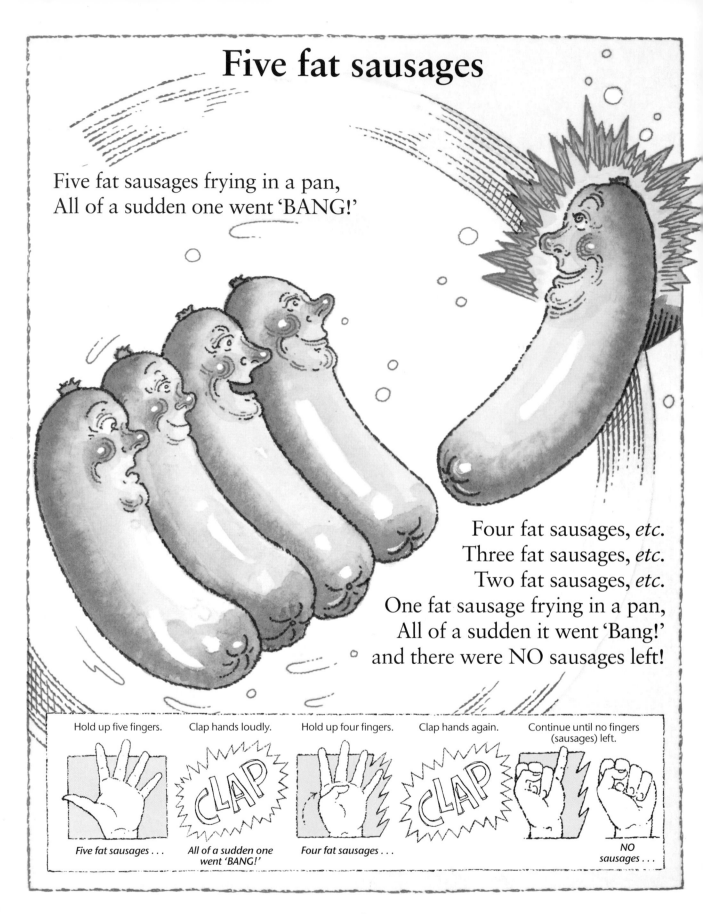

Five fat sausages frying in a pan,
All of a sudden one went 'BANG!'

Four fat sausages, *etc.*
Three fat sausages, *etc.*
Two fat sausages, *etc.*
One fat sausage frying in a pan,
All of a sudden it went 'Bang!'
and there were NO sausages left!

Hold up five fingers.   Clap hands loudly.   Hold up four fingers.   Clap hands again.   Continue until no fingers (sausages) left.

Five fat sausages . . .   *All of a sudden one went 'BANG!'*   *Four fat sausages . . .*   *NO sausages . . .*

Foxy's hole

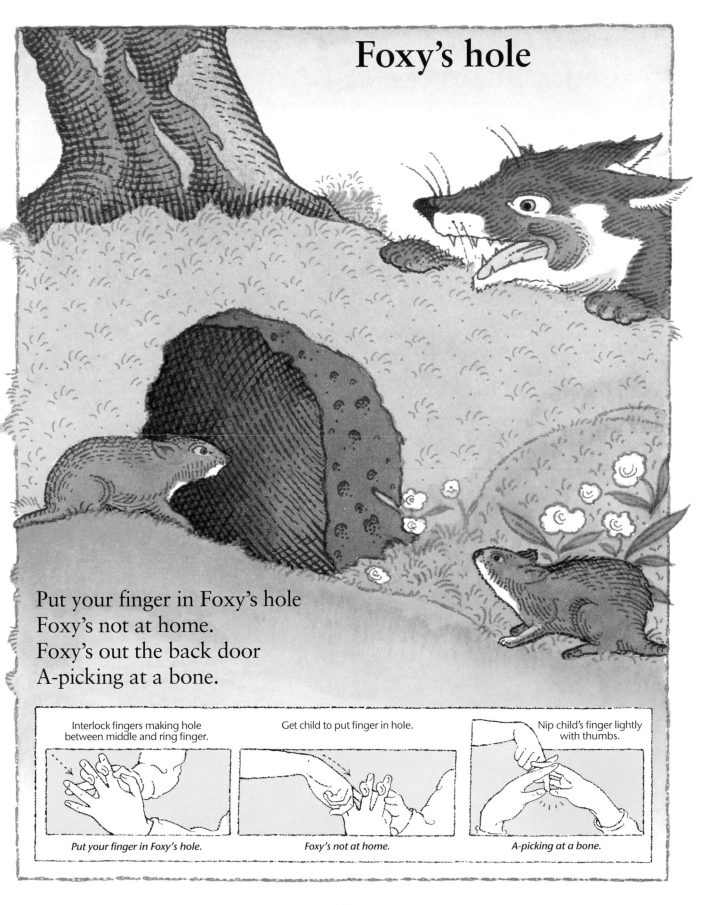

Put your finger in Foxy's hole
Foxy's not at home.
Foxy's out the back door
A-picking at a bone.

Interlock fingers making hole
between middle and ring finger.

Get child to put finger in hole.

Nip child's finger lightly
with thumbs.

Put your finger in Foxy's hole.

Foxy's not at home.

A-picking at a bone.

7

Clap, clap hands

Clap, clap hands, one, two, three,
Put your hands upon your knees,
Lift them high to touch the sky,
Clap, clap hands and away they fly.

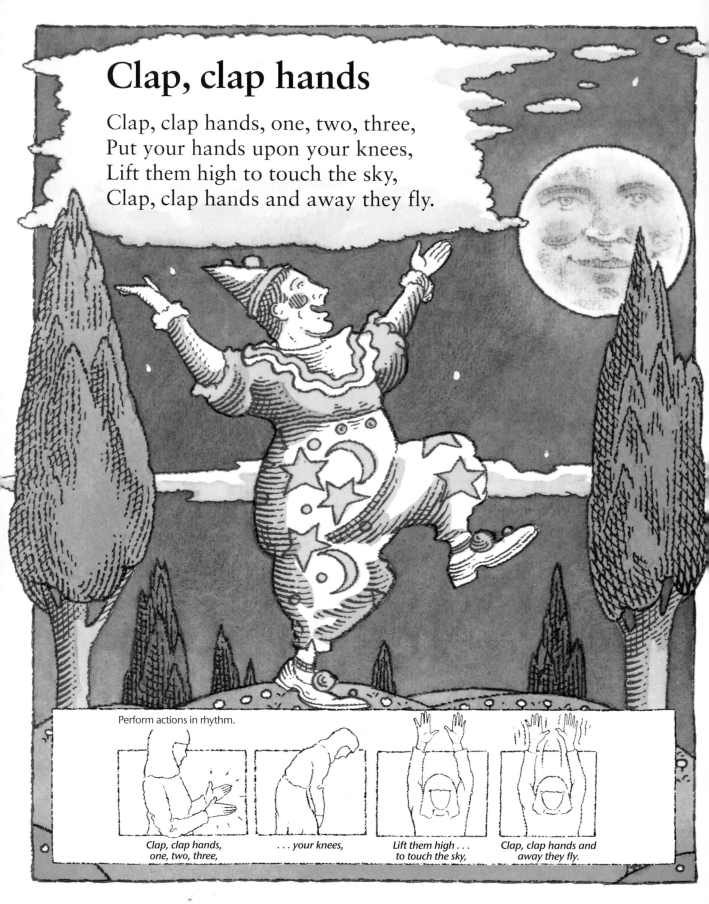

Perform actions in rhythm.

Clap, clap hands,
one, two, three,

. . . your knees,

Lift them high . . .
to touch the sky,

Clap, clap hands and
away they fly.

The apple tree

Here is the tree with leaves so green.

Here are the apples that hang between.

When the wind blows the apples fall.

Here is a basket to gather them all.

Make tree with arms.

Here is the tree . . .

Clench fists.

Here are the apples . . .

Wave arms as if in wind and let fists fall suddenly.

. . . the apples fall.

Make a basket with both hands.

Here is a basket to gather them all.

Piggy on the railway

Piggy on the railway,
Shouldn't be there;
Along came an engine,
Piggy take care!

'Hey!' said the driver,
'Get off the track.'
Piggy ran away then,
And NEVER CAME BACK!

Raise palms in the air.

Move arm forward and round like piston of a steam train.

Raise hands in surprise and anger.

Make walking movements with fingers.

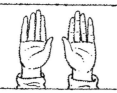

*Piggy on the railway,
Shouldn't be there;*

*Along came an engine,
Piggy take care!*

*'Hey!' said the driver,
'Get off the track.'*

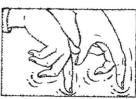

*Piggy ran away then,
AND NEVER CAME BACK!*

Little cottage

Little cottage in a wood,
Little man at a window stood,
Saw a rabbit running by,
Knocking at the door.
'Help me! help me! help me!' he cried,
'See the hunters on their way.'
'Little rabbit, come inside,
You'll be safe with me.'

Make roof of cottage with hands.	Look through hands for window.	Wiggle two fingers.	Knock at door.	Shoot hands upward from shoulders and down while rabbit is talking.	Point for hunters, and beckon.	Stroke hand (rabbit).
Little cottage in a wood,	*Little man at a window stood,*	*. . . rabbit running by,*	*Knocking at the door.*	*'Help me! help me! help me!' he cried,*	*'. . . come inside,*	*You'll be safe with me.'*

My house

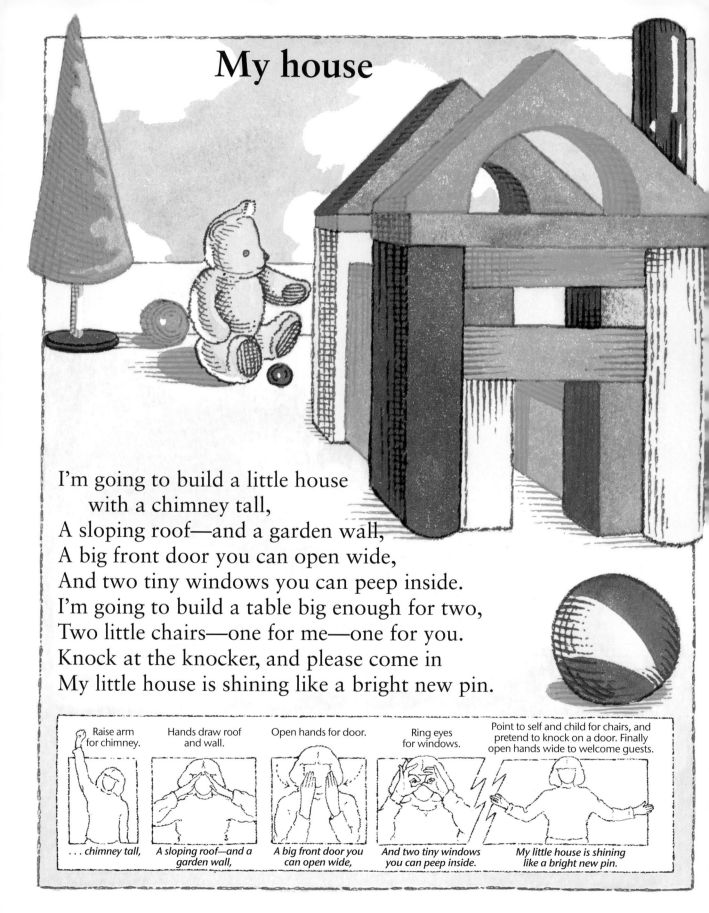

I'm going to build a little house
   with a chimney tall,
A sloping roof—and a garden wall,
A big front door you can open wide,
And two tiny windows you can peep inside.
I'm going to build a table big enough for two,
Two little chairs—one for me—one for you.
Knock at the knocker, and please come in
My little house is shining like a bright new pin.

Raise arm for chimney.	Hands draw roof and wall.	Open hands for door.	Ring eyes for windows.	Point to self and child for chairs, and pretend to knock on a door. Finally open hands wide to welcome guests.
. . . *chimney tall,*	*A sloping roof—and a garden wall,*	*A big front door you can open wide,*	*And two tiny windows you can peep inside.*	*My little house is shining like a bright new pin.*

12

Mousie

Mousie comes a-creeping, creeping.
Mousie comes a-peeping, peeping.
Mousie said, 'I'd like to stay,
But I haven't time today.'
Mousie popped into his hole
And said, 'Achoo!
I've caught a cold!'

Close fist and push index finger of other hand through.

Mousie comes a-creeping, creeping.

Push finger through until tip just appears.

Mousie comes a-peeping, peeping.

Waggle finger.

Mousie said, 'I'd like to stay,'

Pull finger suddenly back and out of sight!

Mousie popped into his hole

Ten little men

Ten little men standing straight,
Ten little men open the gate,
Ten little men all in a ring,
Ten little men bow to the king,
Ten little men dance all day,
Ten little men hide away.

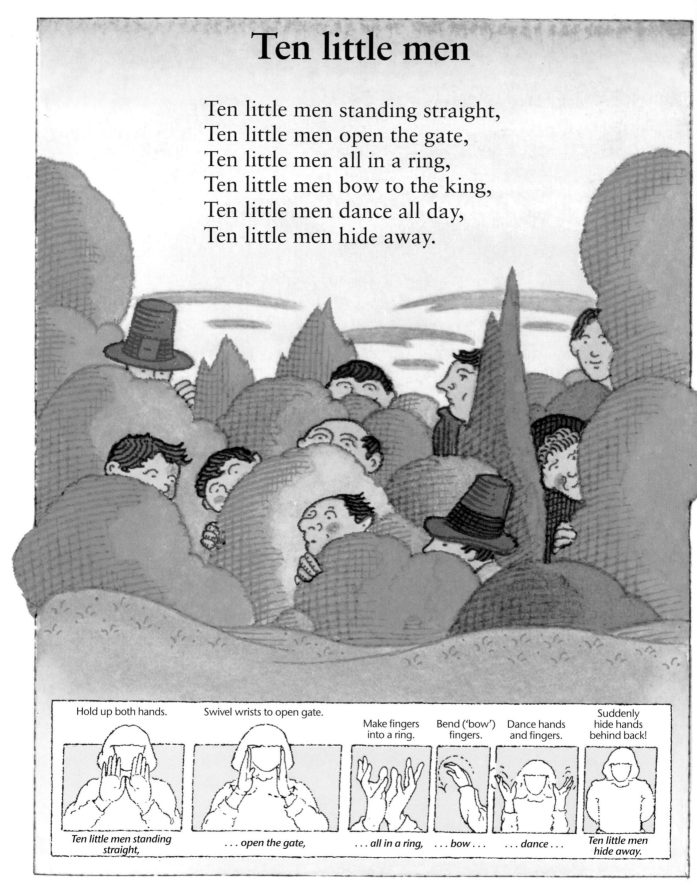

Hold up both hands.

Swivel wrists to open gate.

Make fingers into a ring.

Bend ('bow') fingers.

Dance hands and fingers.

Suddenly hide hands behind back!

Ten little men standing straight,

. . . open the gate,

. . . all in a ring,

. . . bow . . .

. . . dance . . .

Ten little men hide away.

Incy, wincy spider

Incy, wincy spider
Climbing up the spout.
Down came the rain
And washed the spider out.

Out came the sun
And dried up all the rain,
So incy, wincy spider
Climbed up the spout again.

Opposite thumb and index finger climb up each other, alternately.

Show rain falling.

Make a large circle.

Opposite thumb and index finger climb up each other again.

Incy, wincy spider
Climbing up the spout.

Down came the rain

Out came the sun

Climbed up the spout again.

Ten little fingers

I have ten little fingers,
And they all belong to me.
I can make them do things,
Would you like to see?
I can shut them up tight,
Or open them all wide.

Put them all together,
Or make them all hide.
I can make them jump high;
I can make them jump low.
I can fold them quietly,
And hold them all just so.

Hold up hands and wiggle fingers.

Clench fists tightly. Open as wide as possible.

Interlock fingers.

Hands behind back.

Move arms up and down.

Place hands, with palms together, in lap.

I have ten little fingers,

I can shut them up tight,

Put them all together,

Or make them all hide.

. . . jump high . . . jump low . . .

And hold them all just so.

16

Row, row, row your boat

Row, row, row your boat,
Gently down the stream,
Merrily, merrily, merrily, merrily,
Life is but a dream. *Repeat*.

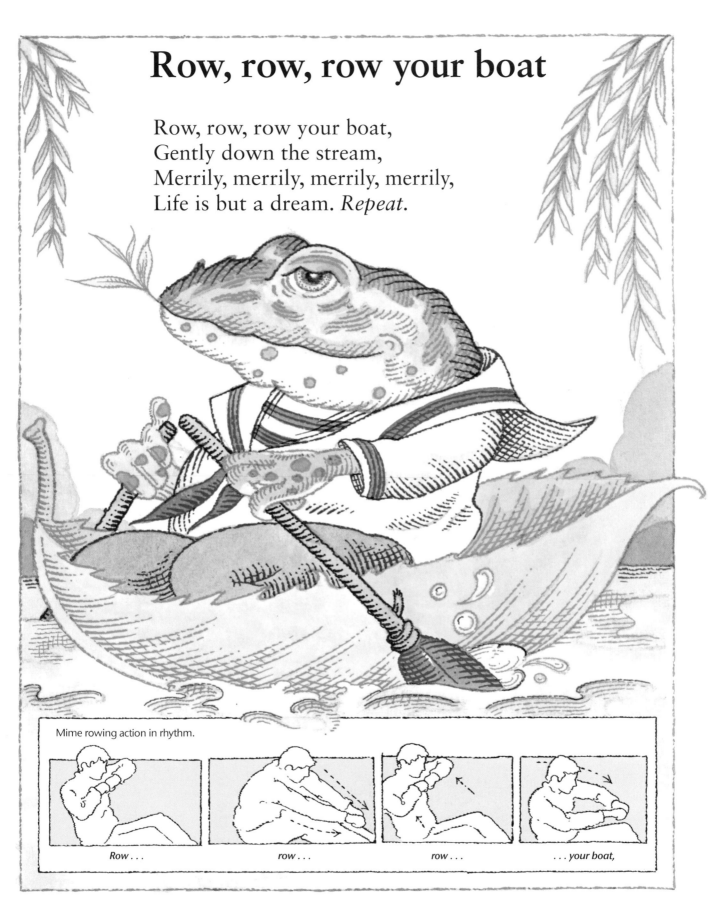

Mime rowing action in rhythm.

Row . . .   *row . . .*   *row . . .*   *. . . your boat,*

Two fat gentlemen

Two fat gentlemen met in a lane,
Bowed most politely, bowed once again.
How do you do? How do you do?
How do you do again?

Two thin ladies met in a lane, *etc.*
Two tall policemen met in a lane, *etc.*
Two little schoolboys met in a lane, *etc.*
Two little babies met in a lane, *etc.*

Hold out fists with thumbs raised.

*Two fat gentlemen
met in a lane,*

Bend each
thumb slowly
forward in turn.

Waggle
each thumb
in turn.

*Bowed most politely,
bowed once again.*

Repeat
actions for
other fingers.

Two thin
ladies = index
fingers, etc.

*How do you do?
How do you do again?*

Here are Grandma's spectacles

Here are Grandma's spectacles,
And here is Grandma's hat,
And here's the way she folds her hands,
And puts them in her lap.

Here are Grandpa's spectacles,
And here is Grandpa's hat,
And here's the way he folds his arms,
And takes a little nap.

Ring eyes for spectacles.	Mime Grandma's hat.	Claps hands lightly and place in lap.	Repeat actions for Grandpa but exaggerate. (e.g. bigger spectacles)
Here are Grandma's spectacles,	*And here is Grandma's hat,*	*And puts them in her lap.*	*And takes a little nap.*

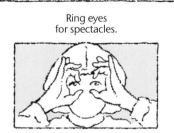

Hickory, dickory, dock

Hickory, dickory, dock,
The mouse ran up the clock,

The clock struck ONE,
The mouse ran down,
Hickory, dickory, dock.

Run fingers lightly up arm.

Clap hands together.

Hickory, dickory, dock,

The mouse ran up the clock,

The clock struck ONE,

Hickory, dickory, dock.

CLAP

Tall shop

Tall shop in the town.
Lifts moving up and down.
Doors swinging round about.
People moving in and out.

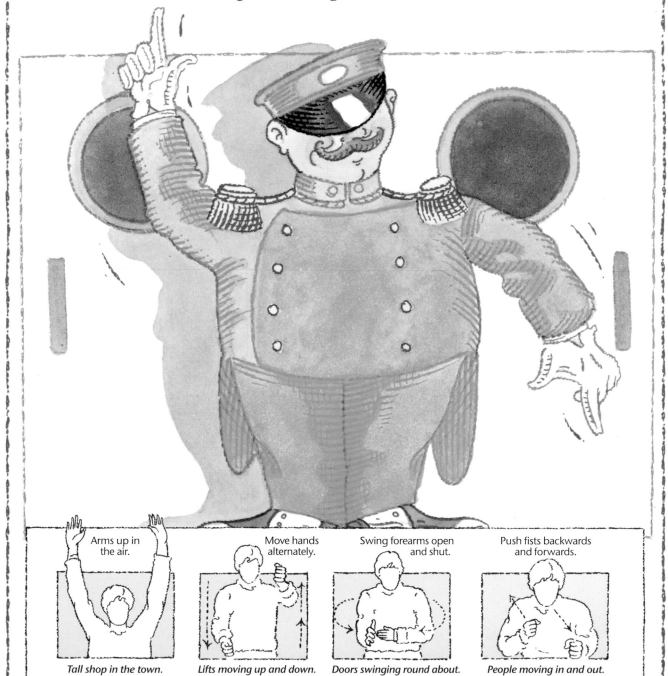

Arms up in the air.	Move hands alternately.	Swing forearms open and shut.	Push fists backwards and forwards.
Tall shop in the town.	*Lifts moving up and down.*	*Doors swinging round about.*	*People moving in and out.*

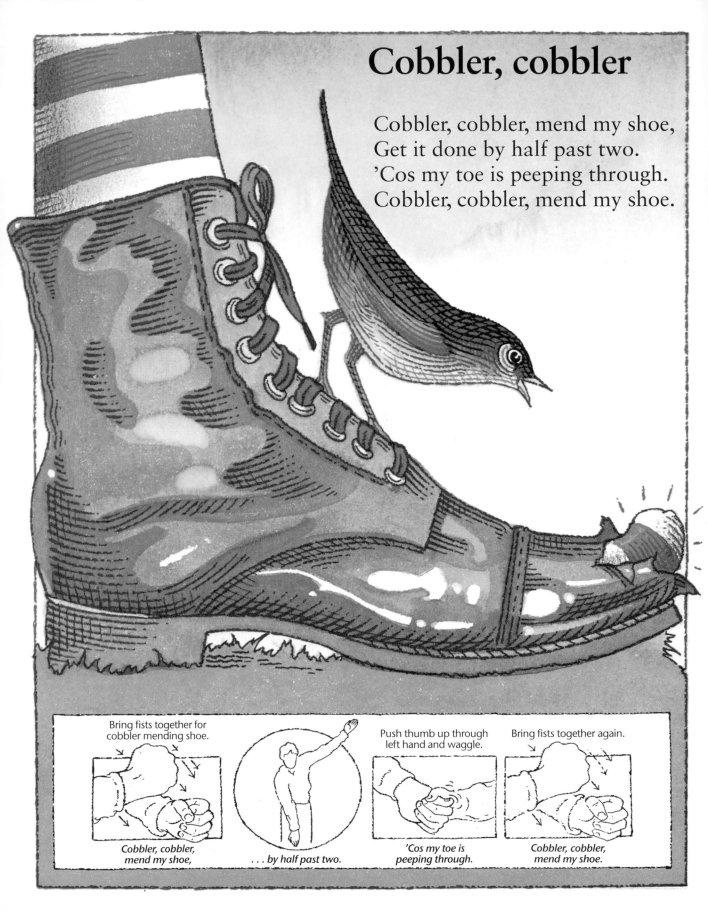

Cobbler, cobbler

Cobbler, cobbler, mend my shoe,
Get it done by half past two.
'Cos my toe is peeping through.
Cobbler, cobbler, mend my shoe.

Bring fists together for cobbler mending shoe.

Cobbler, cobbler, mend my shoe,

. . . by half past two.

Push thumb up through left hand and waggle.

'Cos my toe is peeping through.

Bring fists together again.

Cobbler, cobbler, mend my shoe.

22

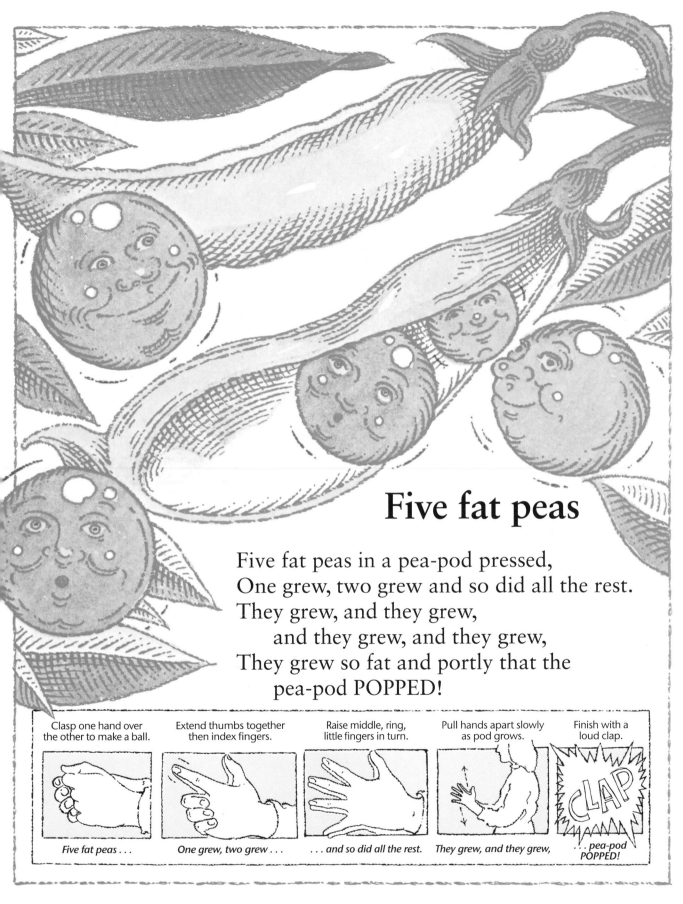

Five fat peas

Five fat peas in a pea-pod pressed,
One grew, two grew and so did all the rest.
They grew, and they grew,
  and they grew, and they grew,
They grew so fat and portly that the
  pea-pod POPPED!

Clasp one hand over the other to make a ball.	Extend thumbs together then index fingers.	Raise middle, ring, little fingers in turn.	Pull hands apart slowly as pod grows.	Finish with a loud clap.
Five fat peas . . .	*One grew, two grew . . .*	*. . . and so did all the rest.*	*They grew, and they grew,*	*. . . pea-pod POPPED!*

23

Knock at the door

Knock at the door,
Peep in,
Lift up the latch,
Walk in.
Chin chopper, chin chopper,
Chin chopper, CHIN!

Tap forehead in rhythm.	Point to eyes.	Tap end of nose in rhythm.	Open mouth, hold finger near.	Tap lightly under chin in rhythm. Finish with sudden tickle on last 'CHIN'.
Knock at the door,	*Peep in,*	*Lift up the latch,*	*Walk in.*	*. . . Chin chopper, CHIN!*

Two little dicky birds

Two little dicky birds
Sitting on a wall.
One named Peter.
One named Paul.
Fly away Peter!
Fly away Paul!
Come back Peter.
Come back Paul.

Stick little piece of paper on each index finger.

Hold out fists with index fingers raised. Shake each finger in turn (Peter, Paul).

Hide each hand behind back. Bring back with middle fingers raised, index fingers hidden.

Hide each hand behind back in turn again. Bring back index fingers raised, middle fingers tucked.

Two little dicky birds
Sitting on a wall.

One named Peter.
One named Paul.

Fly away Peter!
Fly away Paul!

Come back Peter.
Come back Paul.

The beehive

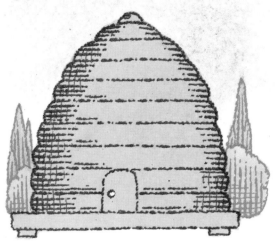

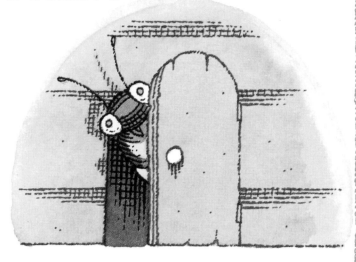

Here is the beehive.
Where are the bees?

Hidden away where nobody sees.

Soon they come creeping out of the hive,
One—two—three, four, five!

Fold hand over other hand to make 'hive'.	Slowly bring fingers, starting with thumb, up and over 'hive'.	Bring last three fingers over 'hive' suddenly and tickle child!
	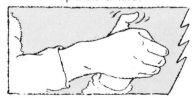	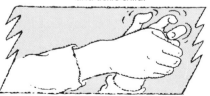
Here is the beehive. *Where are the bees?*	*Soon they come creeping* *out of the hive,*	*. . . three, four, five!*

Tommy Thumb

Tommy Thumb, Tommy Thumb,
Where are you?
Here I am, here I am,
How do you do?

Peter Pointer, *etc.*
Middle Man, *etc.*
Ruby Ring, *etc.*
Baby Small, *etc.*

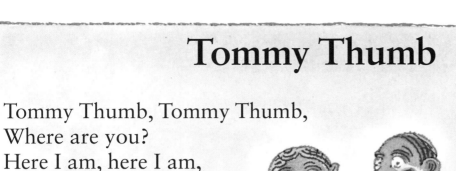

Fingers all, fingers all,
Where are you?
Here we are, here we are,
How do you do?

Make fists and hold them out,
extend thumbs and waggle them.

*Tommy Thumb, Tommy Thumb,
Where are you?*

Continue through all the fingers as with the thumbs:
forefingers, middle fingers, ring fingers, little fingers.

Peter Pointer, etc.

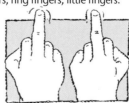

Middle Man, etc.

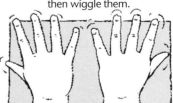

Make fists, extend all fingers and
then wiggle them.

*Fingers all, fingers all,
Where are you?*

This little pig

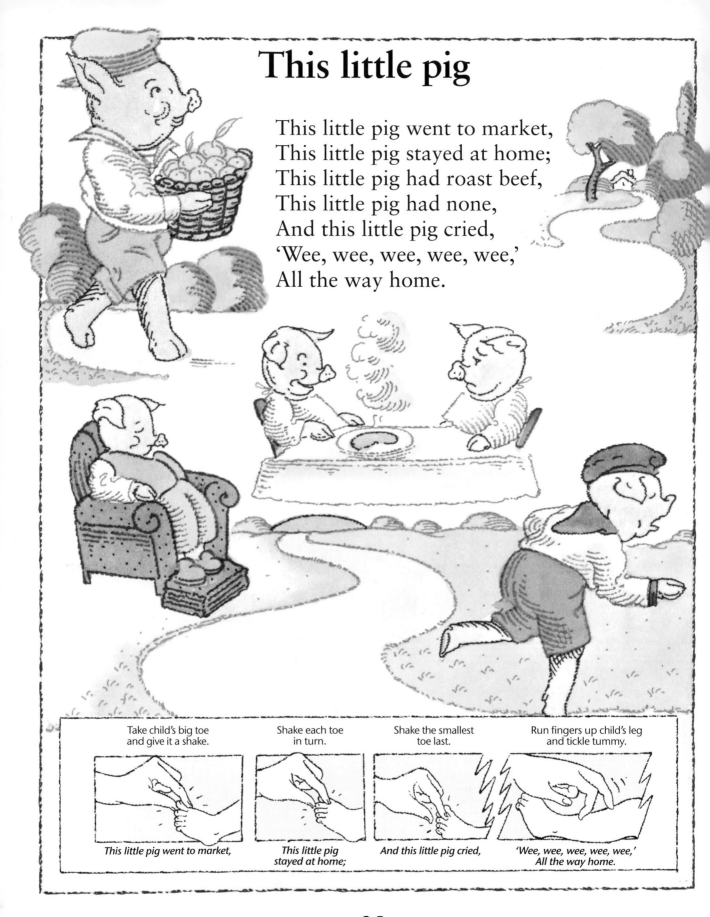

This little pig went to market,
This little pig stayed at home;
This little pig had roast beef,
This little pig had none,
And this little pig cried,
'Wee, wee, wee, wee, wee,'
All the way home.

Take child's big toe and give it a shake.

Shake each toe in turn.

Shake the smallest toe last.

Run fingers up child's leg and tickle tummy.

This little pig went to market,

This little pig stayed at home;

And this little pig cried,

'Wee, wee, wee, wee, wee,' All the way home.

I hear thunder

I hear thunder,
I hear thunder,
Oh! don't you?
Oh! don't you?
Pitter, patter raindrops.
Pitter, patter raindrops.
I'm wet through.
I'm wet through.

I see blue skies.
I see blue skies.
Way up high.
Way up high.
Hurry up the sunshine.
Hurry up the sunshine.
I'll soon dry.
I'll soon dry.

Hands behind ears pretend to listen and point to someone else.

Flutter hands down for rain, then pretend to be wet and finally point up to the sky.

Hands make circular motions in front of chest.

Sweep hands outwards and back.

I hear thunder, . . . Oh! don't you?

Pitter, patter raindrops.

I'm wet through.

Way up high.

Hurry up the sunshine.

I'll soon dry.

To the tune of 'Frère Jacques'.

29

Pat-a-cake

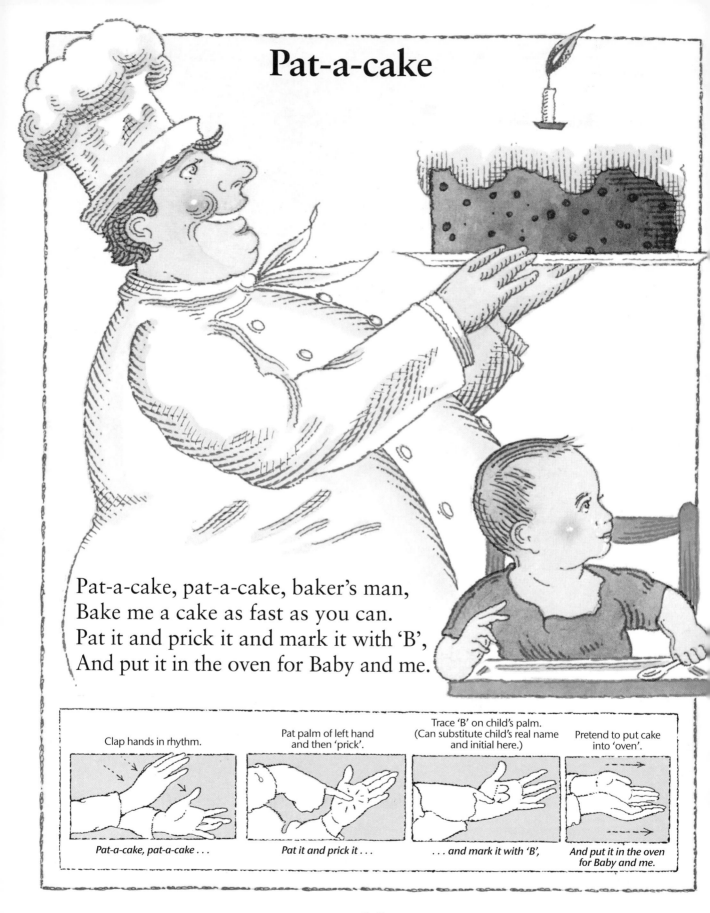

Pat-a-cake, pat-a-cake, baker's man,
Bake me a cake as fast as you can.
Pat it and prick it and mark it with 'B',
And put it in the oven for Baby and me.

Clap hands in rhythm.

Pat-a-cake, pat-a-cake . . .

Pat palm of left hand
and then 'prick'.

Pat it and prick it . . .

Trace 'B' on child's palm.
(Can substitute child's real name
and initial here.)

. . . and mark it with 'B',

Pretend to put cake
into 'oven'.

*And put it in the oven
for Baby and me.*

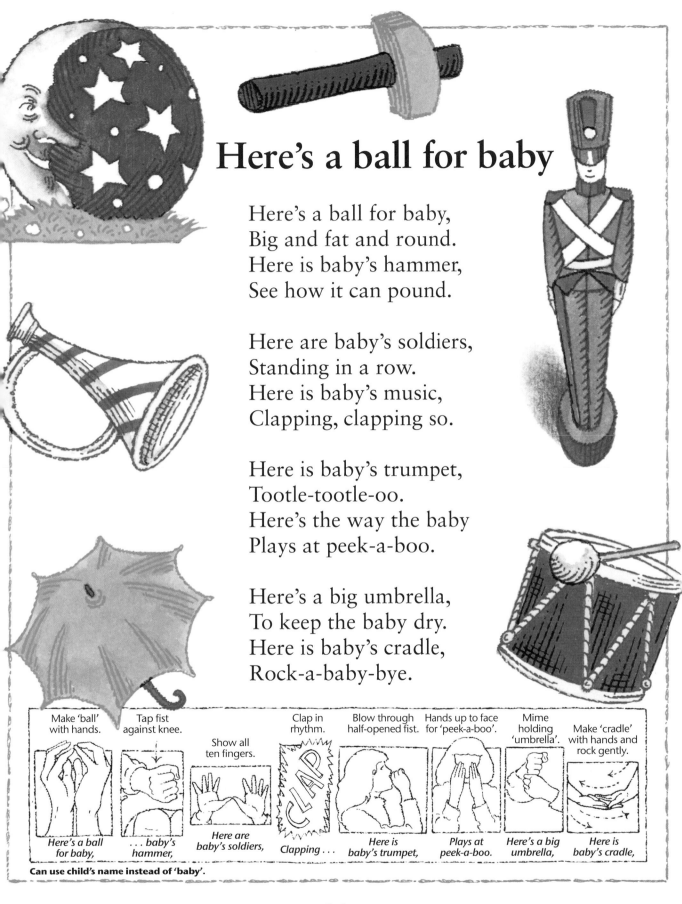

Here's a ball for baby

Here's a ball for baby,
Big and fat and round.
Here is baby's hammer,
See how it can pound.

Here are baby's soldiers,
Standing in a row.
Here is baby's music,
Clapping, clapping so.

Here is baby's trumpet,
Tootle-tootle-oo.
Here's the way the baby
Plays at peek-a-boo.

Here's a big umbrella,
To keep the baby dry.
Here is baby's cradle,
Rock-a-baby-bye.

Make 'ball' with hands.

Tap fist against knee.

Show all ten fingers.

Clap in rhythm.

Blow through half-opened fist.

Hands up to face for 'peek-a-boo'.

Mime holding 'umbrella'.

Make 'cradle' with hands and rock gently.

CLAP

Here's a ball for baby,

... baby's hammer,

Here are baby's soldiers,

Clapping ...

Here is baby's trumpet,

Plays at peek-a-boo.

Here's a big umbrella,

Here is baby's cradle,

Can use child's name instead of 'baby'.

31

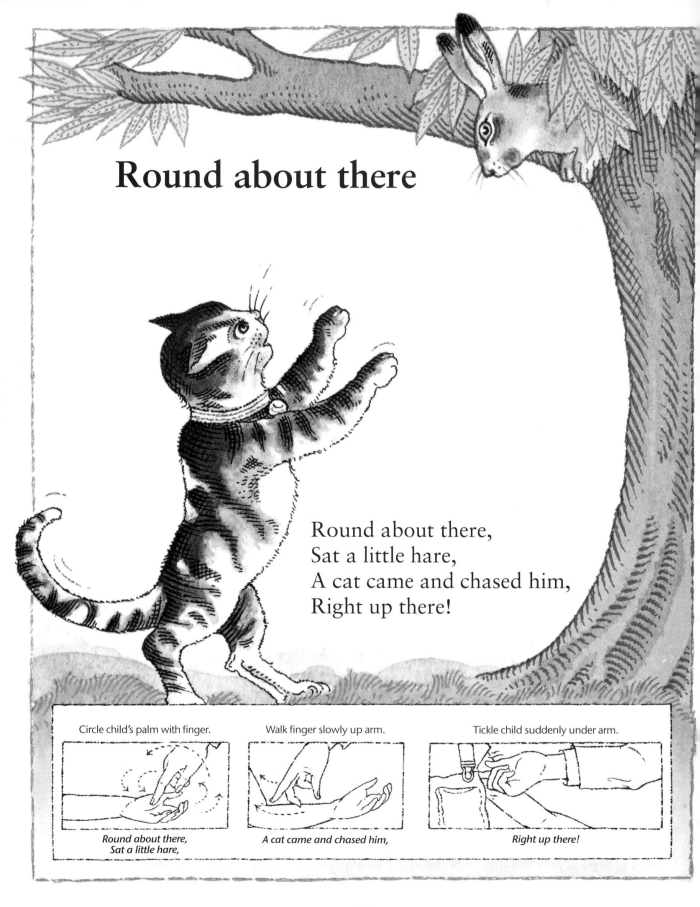

Round about there

Round about there,
Sat a little hare,
A cat came and chased him,
Right up there!

Circle child's palm with finger.

Walk finger slowly up arm.

Tickle child suddenly under arm.

Round about there,
Sat a little hare,

A cat came and chased him,

Right up there!

Here is the church

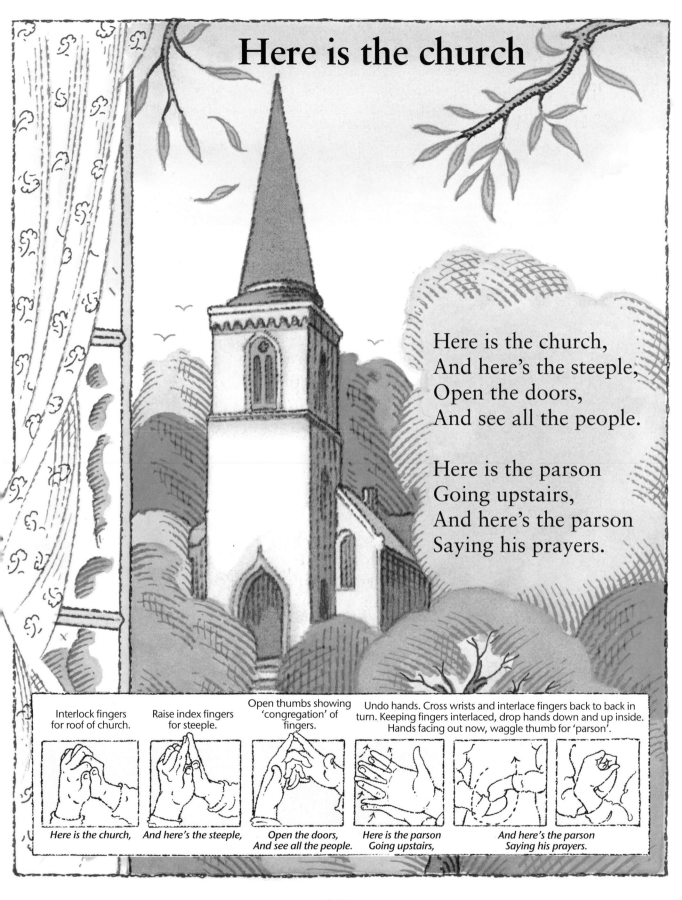

Here is the church,
And here's the steeple,
Open the doors,
And see all the people.

Here is the parson
Going upstairs,
And here's the parson
Saying his prayers.

Interlock fingers for roof of church.

Raise index fingers for steeple.

Open thumbs showing 'congregation' of fingers.

Undo hands. Cross wrists and interlace fingers back to back in turn. Keeping fingers interlaced, drop hands down and up inside. Hands facing out now, waggle thumb for 'parson'.

Here is the church,

And here's the steeple,

Open the doors,
And see all the people.

Here is the parson
Going upstairs,

And here's the parson
Saying his prayers.

Five little soldiers

Five little soldiers standing in a row,
Three stood straight,

And two stood—so.
Along came the captain,
And what do you think?
They ALL stood straight,
As quick as a wink.

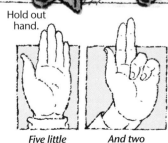

Five little soldiers	And two stood—so.

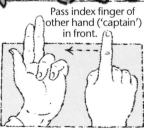

Along came the captain,

And what do you think?

They ALL stood straight,
As quick as a wink.

Hold out hand.

Pass index finger of other hand ('captain') in front.

As index finger passes, straighten fingers.

The cherry tree

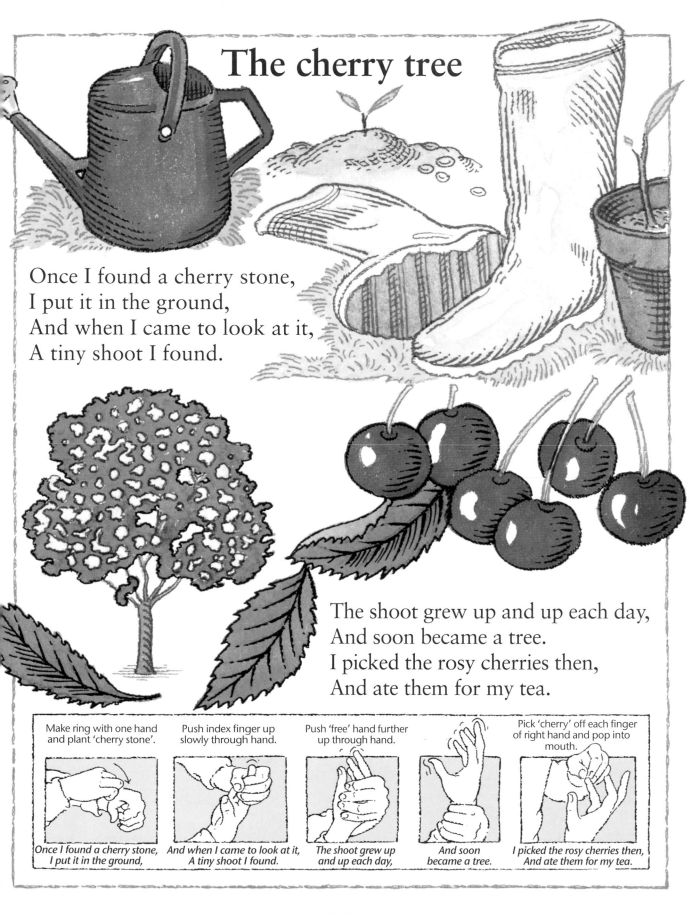

Once I found a cherry stone,
I put it in the ground,
And when I came to look at it,
A tiny shoot I found.

The shoot grew up and up each day,
And soon became a tree.
I picked the rosy cherries then,
And ate them for my tea.

Make ring with one hand and plant 'cherry stone'.

Push index finger up slowly through hand.

Push 'free' hand further up through hand.

Pick 'cherry' off each finger of right hand and pop into mouth.

Once I found a cherry stone,
I put it in the ground,

And when I came to look at it,
A tiny shoot I found.

The shoot grew up
and up each day,

And soon
became a tree.

I picked the rosy cherries then,
And ate them for my tea.

35

Five brown teddies

1. Five brown teddies sitting on a wall.
   Five brown teddies sitting on a wall.
   And if one brown teddy should accidentally fall,
   There'd be four brown teddies sitting on a wall.

2. Four brown teddies sitting on a wall, *etc*.
3. Three brown teddies sitting on a wall, *etc*.
4. Two brown teddies sitting on a wall, *etc*.
5. One brown teddy sitting on a wall.
   And if one brown teddy should accidentally fall,
   There'd be no brown teddies sitting there at all!

TODAY

5

CIRCUS

TEDDINIS

- **Age:** 2–4
- **Number of children:** five

Five brown teddies instructions

This song has the same tune as 'Ten Green Bottles', and is just right for younger children to learn. You can alter the number of children as required, though remember that any number over five can be a little difficult for the younger ones to cope with.

Choose five chilren and place them, sitting in a row. Everybody sings together. On the first verse, one child gently falls backwards, and lies there until the end of the song. On the second verse, the next child does the same, and so on, until they are all lying down.

Five brown ted - dies sit - ting on a wall. Five brown ted - dies

sit - ting on a wall. And if one brown ted - dy should

ac - ci - dent - ally fall, There'd be four brown ted - dies sit - ting on a wall.

(Guitarists may prefer to capo up 3 frets and play in key of D. Use chords D, A7 and G.)

Here we go round the mulberry bush

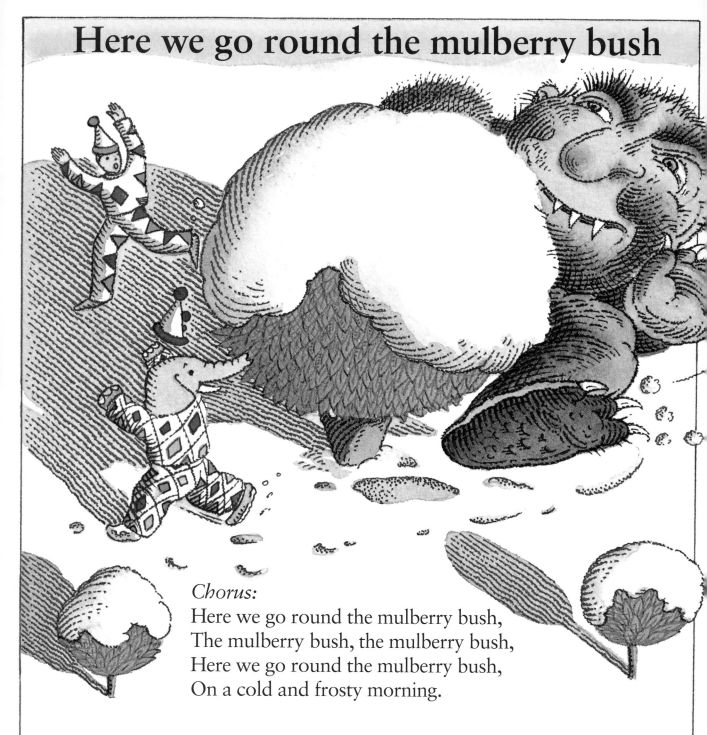

Chorus:
Here we go round the mulberry bush,
The mulberry bush, the mulberry bush,
Here we go round the mulberry bush,
On a cold and frosty morning.

1. This is the way we wash our face,
Wash our face, wash our face,
This is the way we wash our face,
On a cold and frosty morning.

2. This is the way we brush our hair, *etc*.
3. This is the way we clean our teeth, *etc*.
4. This is the way we put on our clothes, *etc*.

(Remember to repeat the chorus after each verse.)

Here we go round the mulberry bush instructions

A good group song which children particularly enjoy as they can suggest their own verses and the tune is very easy to learn. Remember to start circling again when singing the chorus after each verse.

1. Form a ring, join hands and walk or skip round singing the chorus.

Here we go round the mulberry bush . . .

2. Stop circling and pretend to wash face.

This is the way we wash our face . . .

3. Stop circling and pretend to brush hair.

. . . brush our hair . . .

4. Stop circling and pretend to brush teeth.

. . . clean our teeth . . .

5. Stop circling and put socks on – jumper, trousers, socks, *etc.*

. . . put on our clothes . . .

Here we go round the mul - berry bush, the mul - berry bush, the mul - berry bush,

Here we go round the mul - berry bush, on a cold and fro - sty morn - ing.

Noah's Ark

Chorus:
Who built the Ark?
Noah! Noah!
Who built the Ark?
Brother Noah built the Ark.

1. Now in came the animals two by two,
   The hippopotamus and the kangaroo.

2. Now in came the animals four by four,
   Two through the window and two through the door.

3. Now in came the animals six by six,
   The elephants laughed at the monkeys' tricks.

4. Now in came the animals eight by eight,
   Some were on time and some were late.

5. Now in came the animals ten by ten,
   Five black roosters and five black hens.

6. Now Noah said: 'Go and shut that door!
   The rain's started falling and we can't take any more!'

(Remember to repeat the chorus after each verse.)

Noah's Ark instructions

- **Age:** 4+
- **Number of children:** any

This song is very good for counting practice, and introduces children to the lovely old Bible story. If you are singing this with a group of children, choose beforehand the child who is to slam a door on the last verse. If you have heavy doors, or glass doors, it is much safer to have an imaginary one!

1. Everyone sings the chorus while putting one fist on top of the other to 'build' the Ark. The chorus is sung and the Ark built after each verse.

Who built the Ark? Noah! Noah! . . .

2. Hold two fingers up on one hand.

Now in came the animals two by two . . .

3. Hold up four fingers, then point to a window and a door with the other hand.

Now in came the animals four by four, two through the window and two through the door . . .

4. Hold up six fingers, then laugh soundlessly while tickling yourself under the arms like a monkey.

Now in came the animals six by six, the elephants laughed at the monkeys' tricks . . .

5. Hold up eight fingers, then look and point to wristwatch (real or imaginary).

Now in came the animals eight by eight, some were on time and some were late . . .

6. Hold up ten fingers, then put them down. Hold up five for the roosters, then five for the hens.

Now in came the animals ten by ten, five black roosters and five black hens . . .

Who built the Ark? No - ah! No - ah! Who built the Ark? Bro - ther
No - ah! built the Ark. 1. Now in came the an - i - mals two, by two The
hip - po - pot - a - mus and the kan - ga - roo

41

Looby-loo

Chorus:
Here we go looby-loo
Here we go looby-light
Here we go looby-loo
All on a Saturday night!

1. Put you right hand in
   Put your right hand out
   Shake it a little, a little
   And turn yourself about.

2. Put your left hand in, *etc.*
3. Put your right foot in, *etc.*
4. Put your left foot in, *etc.*
5. Put your whole self in, *etc.*

(Remember to repeat the chorus after each verse.)

Looby-loo instructions

This lovely dancing song is a good way of introducing the concept of left and right to young children. Don't worry, however, if the very young ones don't get it right; let them simply enjoy the actions of moving and shaking themselves about!
Form a circle, join hands, and dance or skip around each time the chorus is sung.
Perform the actions as described in the verses.

Everybody dances round during the chorus and does the appropriate actions during the verses.

Here we go looby-loo . . .

Here we go loo-by-loo, Here we go loo-by-light
Here we go loo-by-loo, All on a Sat-ur-day night.
1. Put your right hand in, Put your right hand out, Shake it a lit-tle, a
lit-tle, And turn — your-self- a- bout.

The grand old Duke of York

1. Oh, the grand old Duke of York,
   He had ten thousand men.
   He marched them up to the top of the hill
   And he marched them down again.

   Chorus:
   And when they were up they were up,
   And when they were down they were down,
   And when they were only halfway up
   They were neither up nor down.

2. Oh, the grand old Duke of York,
   He had ten thousand men.
   They beat their drums to the top of the hill
   And they beat them down again.

3. They played their pipes to the top of the hill,

4. They banged their guns to the top of the hill,

The grand old Duke of York **instructions**

- **Age:** 2½–5
- **Number of children:** any

If you are in a large room, you can march across to one side of the room for the top of the hill; back to the other side for the bottom; and in the middle for half-way up. This is noisy, and the song won't be sung smoothly, but it is more realistic, and children enjoy pretending to be soldiers marching along. Alternatively everyone can use their fingers to make all the marching actions.

1. Everyone sing together and march across the room and back again.

He marched them up to the top of the hill and he marched them down again . . .

2. All stand up.

And when they were up, they were up,

3. All sit down.

And when they were down, they were down,

4. All crouch halfway between standing and sitting. Stand up again. Sit down again.

And when they were only halfway up They were neither up nor down.

Oh, the grand old Duke of York, He had ten thou-sand men, He marched them up to the top of the hill And he marched them down a-gain. And when they were up they were up, And when they were down they were down. And when they were on-ly half-way up They were nei-ther up nor down.

Ring-a-ring o'roses

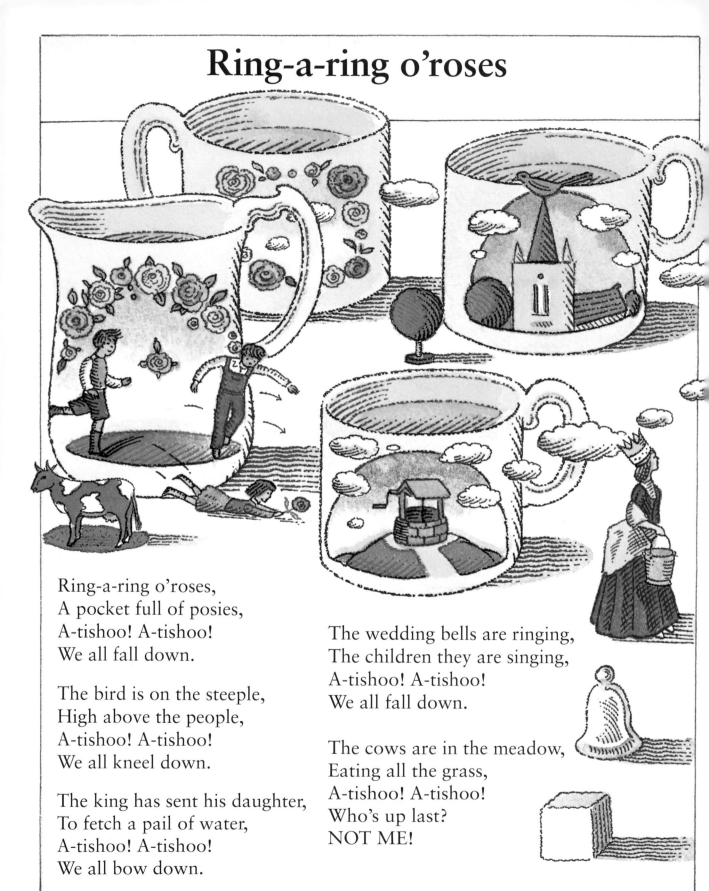

Ring-a-ring o'roses,
A pocket full of posies,
A-tishoo! A-tishoo!
We all fall down.

The bird is on the steeple,
High above the people,
A-tishoo! A-tishoo!
We all kneel down.

The king has sent his daughter,
To fetch a pail of water,
A-tishoo! A-tishoo!
We all bow down.

The wedding bells are ringing,
The children they are singing,
A-tishoo! A-tishoo!
We all fall down.

The cows are in the meadow,
Eating all the grass,
A-tishoo! A-tishoo!
Who's up last?
NOT ME!

Ring-a-ring o'roses instructions

This is so popular that it hardly needs an introduction. It can be played with the tiniest toddlers, who will probably be happy with the first verse over and over again! The extra verses add more interest for older children.

1. Make a ring, link hands and circle singing each verse together.

Ring-a-ring o'roses . . .

2. Bump down on to floor on the word 'down'.

. . . A-tishoo! A-tishoo! We all fall down.

5. Bump down again on the word 'down'. Stay down until last line of next verse.

3. Kneel down on the word 'kneel'.

. . . A-tishoo! A-tishoo! We all kneel down.

6-7. Turn on all fours and pretend to be a cow chewing the cud. Leap up quickly on to feet and shout 'NOT ME!'

. . . A-tishoo! A-tishoo! Who's up last? NOT ME!

4. Bow as if to the king, on the word 'bow'.

. . . A-tishoo! A-tishoo! We all bow down.

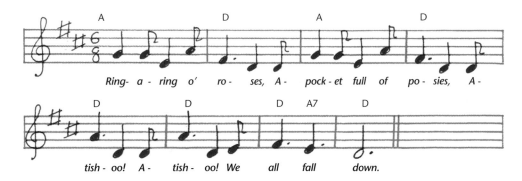

Ring- a - ring o' ro - ses, A - pock - et full of po - sies, A - tish - oo! A - tish - oo! We all fall down.

The farmer's in his den

1. The farmer's in his den,
   The farmer's in his den.
   Eee-aye-eee-aye,
   The farmer's in his den.
2. The farmer wants a wife, *etc.*
3. The wife wants a child, *etc.*
4. The child wants a nurse, *etc.*
5. The nurse wants a dog, *etc.*
6. The dog wants a bone, *etc.*
7. We all clap the bone, *etc.*

The farmer's in his den instructions

- **Age:** 3+
- **Number of children:** ten or more

On the last verse I have used 'clap the bone', instead of the more traditional 'pat the bone'. If you use the latter, however, the the 'bone' is *gently* patted on the head. I emphasise 'gently', as the 'bone' can get hurt if everyone pats him too enthusiastically!

1. Choose a child to be a farmer, The farmer stands in the centre of a circling ring of children. Everybody sings.

The farmer's in his den . . .

2. The farmer chooses a child from the ring to be his wife. She joins him in the centre.

The farmer wants a wife . . .

3. The child, nurse, dog, and bone are selected in turn, and then everyone gathers around the bone, clapping hands in time to the tune.

We all clap the bone . . .

1. The far-mer's in his den, The far-mer's in his den.

Ee-aye-ee-aye, The far-mer's in his den.

49

Five little speckled frogs

1. Five little speckled frogs
   Sat on a speckled log,
   Eating some most delicious bugs,
   Yum! Yum!
   One jumped into the pool,
   Where it was nice and cool,
   Now there are four more
      speckled frogs, Glub! Glub!

2. Four little speckled frogs, *etc.*
3. Three little speckled frogs, *etc.*
4. Two little speckled frogs, *etc.*
5. One little speckled frog, *etc* . . .
   . . . Now there are no more
   speckled frogs, Glub! Glub!

Five little
speckled frogs instructions

• **Age:** 3+
• **Number of children:** any

This is an action song game for younger children. If you have a large number of children, they can be divided into groups of five, one group being 'frogs' first, while the others sing and count. The number of frogs can be adapted to three, four, six, or any number you like. Remember not to have too high a number with young children.

1. Choose five children and place them, squatting, in a well-spaced ring. Everybody sings the song together.

2. Each child pretends to eat with one hand and rub tummy with the other.

3. One child leaps into the centre of the ring, and remains there until end of song. On each verse, thereafter, one more child leaps into the 'pool', until no more are left in the ring.

Five little speckled frogs sat on a speckled log . . .

. . . Eating some most delicious bugs, Yum! Yum!

One jumped into the pool . . .

Five lit - tle spe - ckled frogs, Sat on a spe - ckled log, Eat - ing some
One jumped in - to the pool, Where it was nice and cool, Now there are

most de - li - cious bugs, Yum! Yum!
four more spe - ckled   frogs, Glub! Glub!

The wheels on the bus

1. The wheels on the bus go round and round,
   Round and round, round and round.
   The wheels on the bus go round and round,
   All day long.

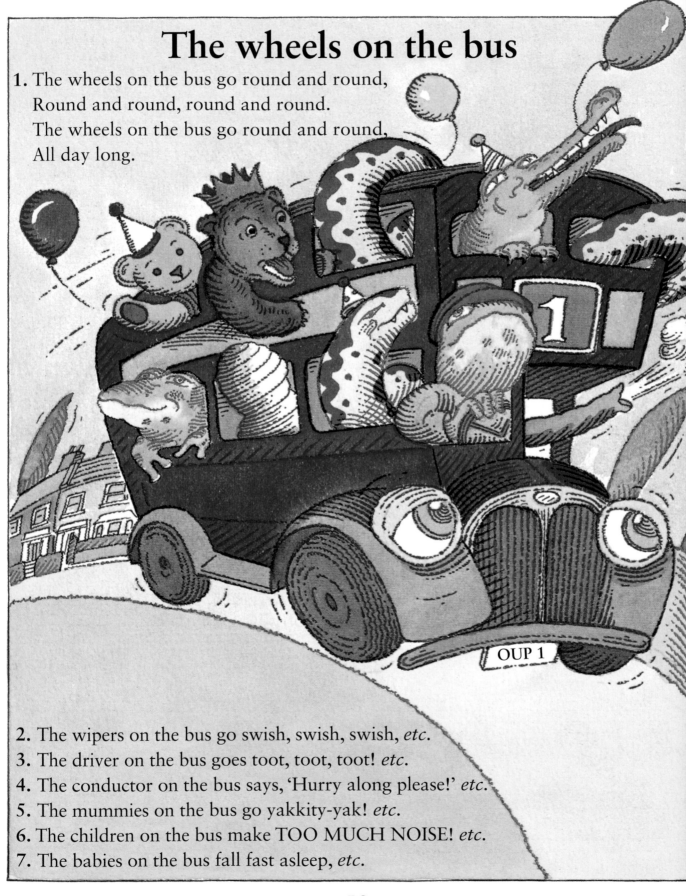

OUP 1

2. The wipers on the bus go swish, swish, swish, *etc.*
3. The driver on the bus goes toot, toot, toot! *etc.*
4. The conductor on the bus says, 'Hurry along please!' *etc.*
5. The mummies on the bus go yakkity-yak! *etc.*
6. The children on the bus make TOO MUCH NOISE! *etc.*
7. The babies on the bus fall fast asleep, *etc.*

The wheels on the bus instructions

- **Age:** 2½+
- **Number of children:** eight or more

A good action song which requires little space. Once learned younger children refuse to get fed up with it. Remember to use the 'babies on the bus' *after* 'the children on the bus' if you want to quieten an over-enthusiastic lot down.

1. All stand (or sit) and sing and perform actions together. Bend arms at elbows and keeping close to sides, hold hands straight out in front. Then rotate arms as if wheels.

The wheels on the bus . . .

2. Hold up hands in front of face, palms facing outwards. Sway hands from left to right for wipers.

The wipers on the bus . . .

3. Make a fist with hand and jab imaginary horn button with thumb.

The driver on the bus . . .

4. Pretend to gently guide a passenger along.

The conductor on the bus . . .

5. Open and shut hands rhythmically as if they are mouths chattering. Sing louder for 'yakkity-yak!'

The mummies on the bus . . .

6. Put both hands over ears and screw up face as if you can't bear the noise. Shout at the top of voice for 'TOO MUCH NOISE'.

The children on the bus . . .

7. Pretend to go to sleep. Sing this verse quietly.

The babies on the bus . . .

The wheels on the bus go round and round, Round and round, round and round. The wheels on the bus go round and round, All day long.

BUS STOP

Boys and girls come out to play

Boys and girls come out to play,
The moon doth shine as bright as day.
Leave your supper and leave your sleep,
And join your playfellows in the street.

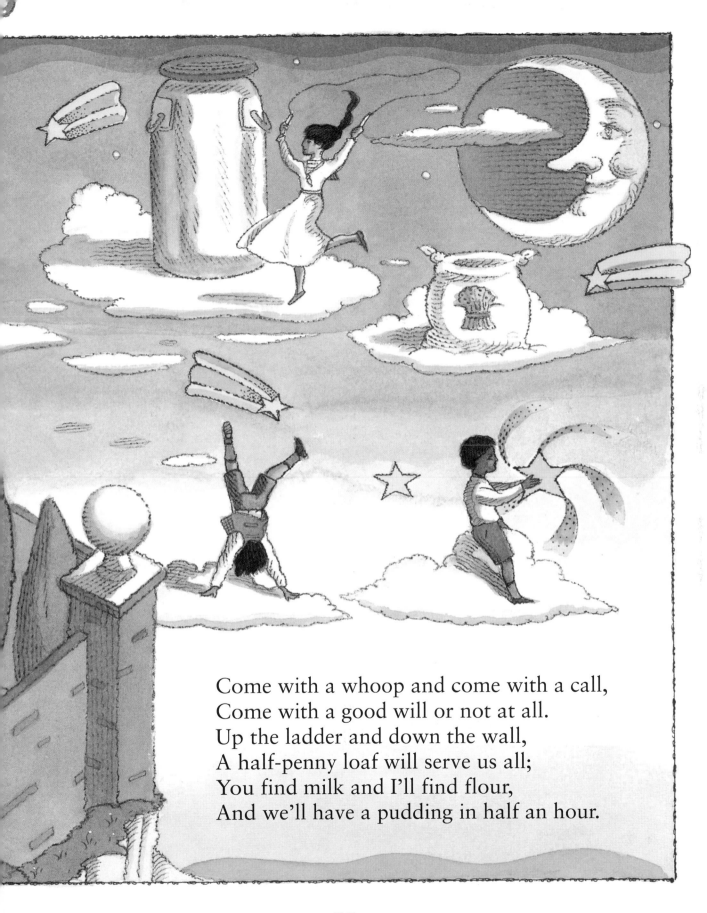

Come with a whoop and come with a call,
Come with a good will or not at all.
Up the ladder and down the wall,
A half-penny loaf will serve us all;
You find milk and I'll find flour,
And we'll have a pudding in half an hour.

There was an old woman

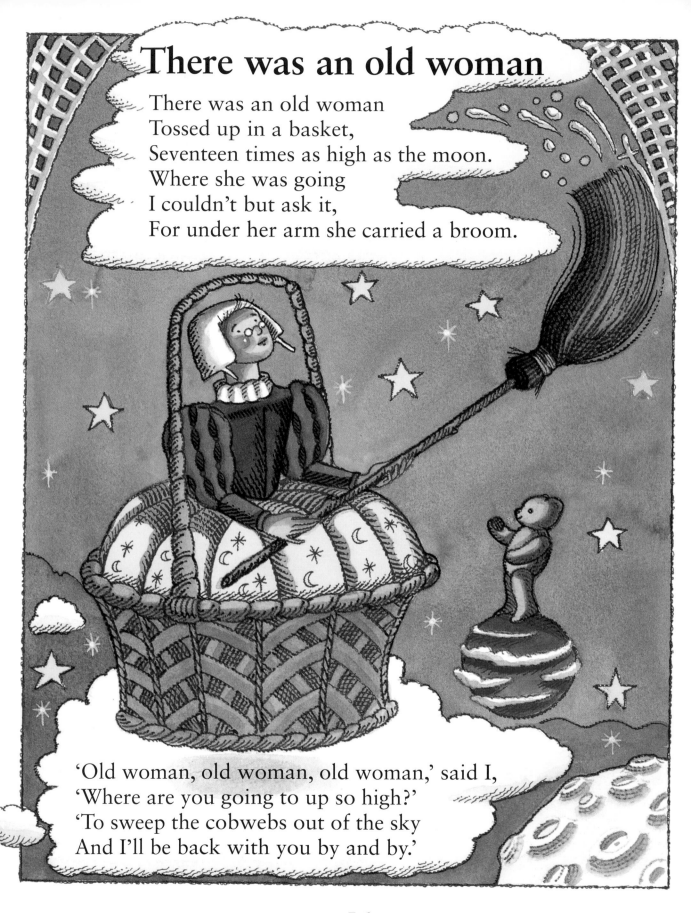

There was an old woman
Tossed up in a basket,
Seventeen times as high as the moon.
Where she was going
I couldn't but ask it,
For under her arm she carried a broom.

'Old woman, old woman, old woman,' said I,
'Where are you going to up so high?'
'To sweep the cobwebs out of the sky
And I'll be back with you by and by.'

Little Miss Muffet

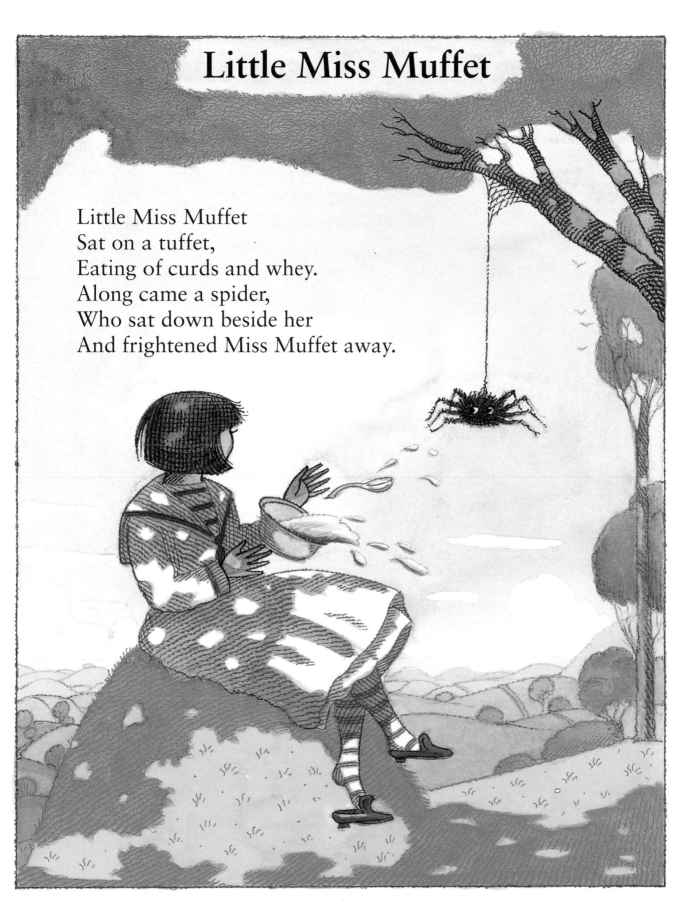

Little Miss Muffet
Sat on a tuffet,
Eating of curds and whey.
Along came a spider,
Who sat down beside her
And frightened Miss Muffet away.

Pudding and pie

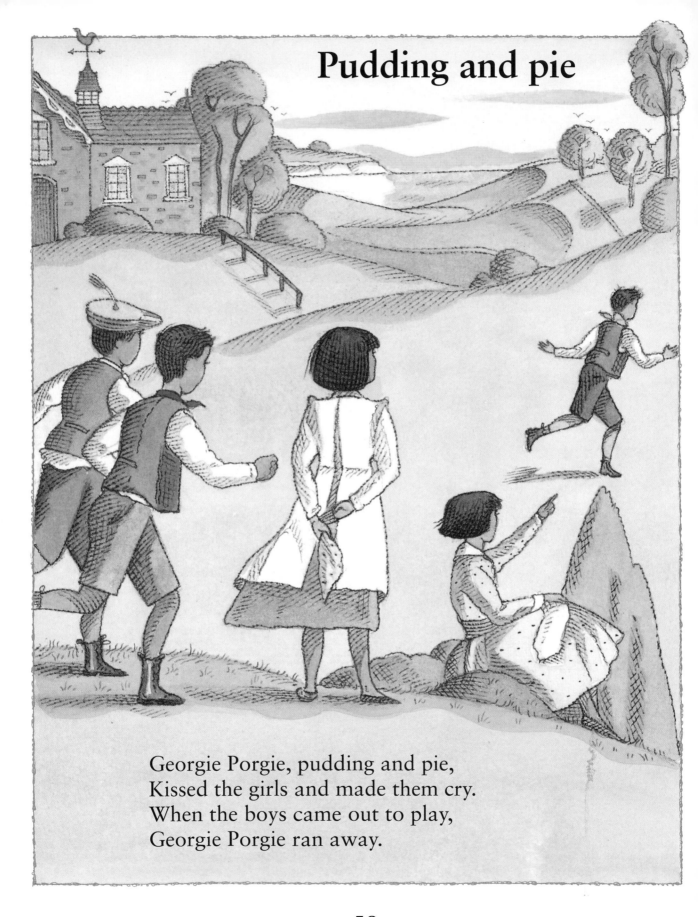

Georgie Porgie, pudding and pie,
Kissed the girls and made them cry.
When the boys came out to play,
Georgie Porgie ran away.

Mary had a little lamb

Mary had a little lamb
Its fleece was white as snow,
And everywhere that Mary went
The lamb was sure to go.

It followed her to school one day,
Which was against the rule.
It made the children laugh and play
To see a lamb at school.

Baa, baa, black sheep

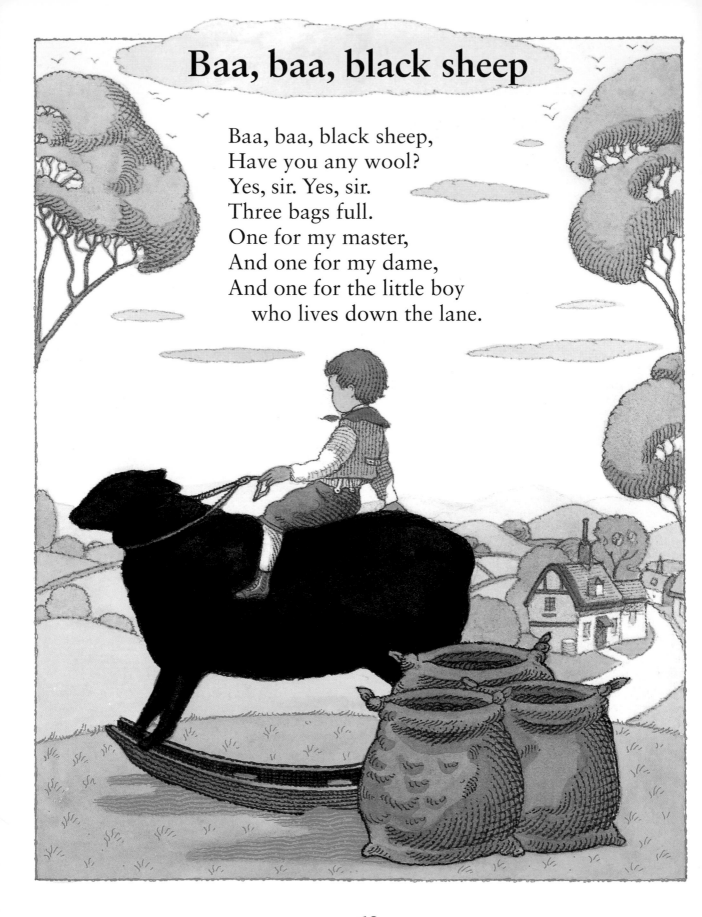

Baa, baa, black sheep,
Have you any wool?
Yes, sir. Yes, sir.
Three bags full.
One for my master,
And one for my dame,
And one for the little boy
   who lives down the lane.

Humpty Dumpty

Humpty Dumpty sat on a wall,
Humpty Dumpty had a great fall;
All the King's horses and all the King's men
Couldn't put Humpty together again.

Old King Cole

Old King Cole
Was a merry old soul,
And a merry old soul was he;
He called for his pipe,
And he called for his bowl,
And he called for his fiddlers three.

Every fiddler had a fine fiddle,
And a very fine fiddle had he;
Fee, fiddledee, fiddledee,
Went the fiddlers.
Oh! There's none so rare,
As can compare
With King Cole and his fiddlers three!

Pussy cat, pussy cat

Pussy cat, pussy cat,
Where have you been?
I've been to London
    to look at the Queen.

Pussy cat, pussy cat,
How did you go?
Oh! I just took a motor car
    over the snow.

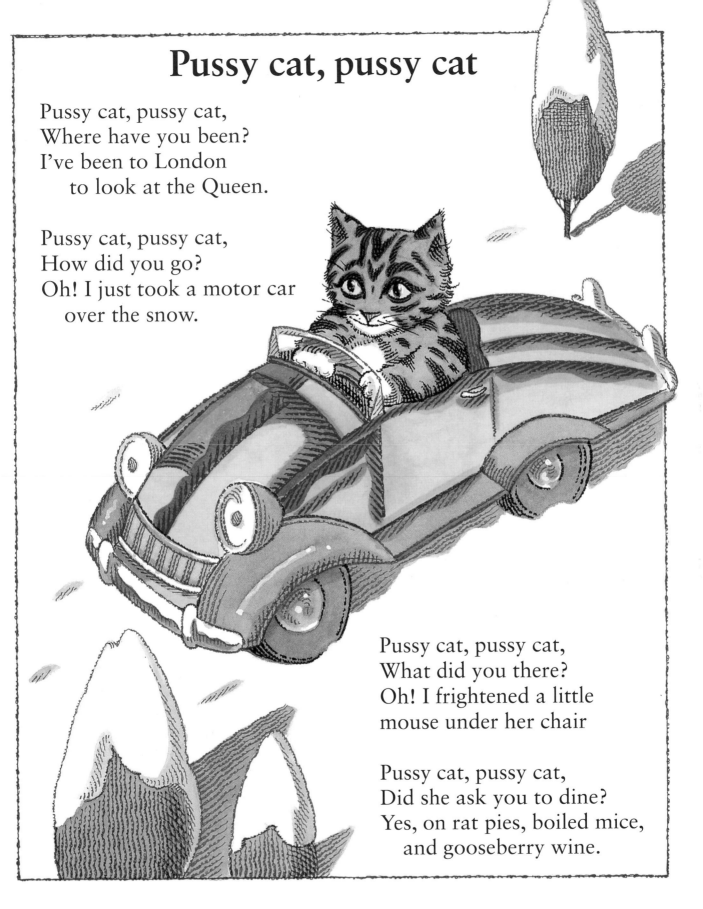

Pussy cat, pussy cat,
What did you there?
Oh! I frightened a little
mouse under her chair

Pussy cat, pussy cat,
Did she ask you to dine?
Yes, on rat pies, boiled mice,
    and gooseberry wine.

How many miles to Babylon?

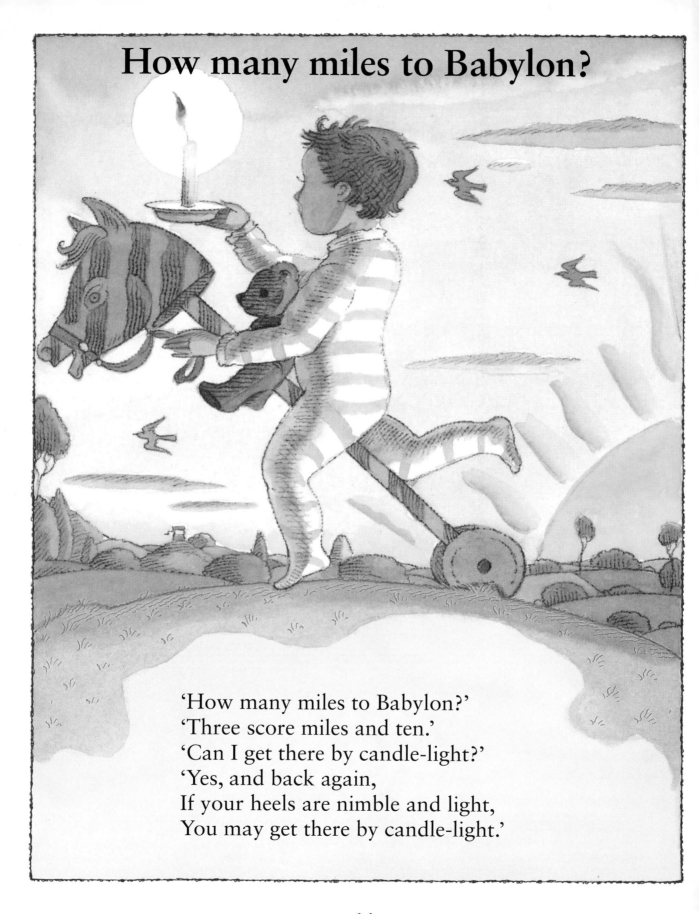

'How many miles to Babylon?'
'Three score miles and ten.'
'Can I get there by candle-light?'
'Yes, and back again,
If your heels are nimble and light,
You may get there by candle-light.'

The Queen of Hearts

The Queen of Hearts
She made some tarts,
All on a summer's day.

The Knave of Hearts
He stole those tarts,
And took them clean away.

The King of Hearts
Called for the tarts,
And beat the knave full sore.

The Knave of Hearts
Brought back the tarts,
And vowed he'd steal no more.

I had a little nut tree

I had a little nut tree,
Nothing would it bear,
But a silver nutmeg
And a golden pear.
The King of Spain's daughter
Came to visit me,
And all for the sake
Of my little nut tree.
I skipped over water,
I danced over sea,
And all the birds in the air
Couldn't catch me.

Mary, Mary

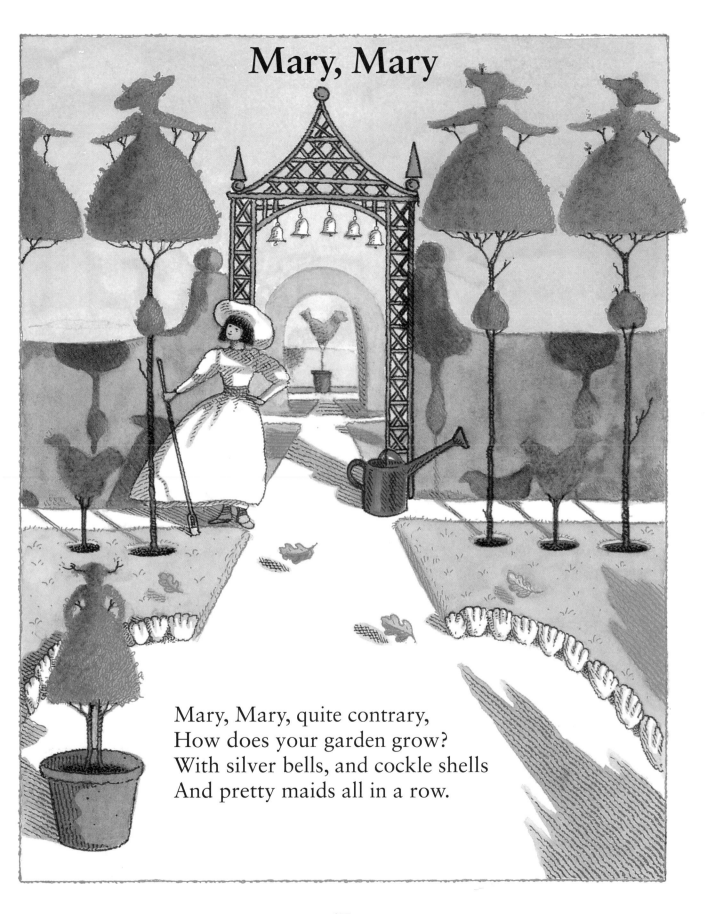

Mary, Mary, quite contrary,
How does your garden grow?
With silver bells, and cockle shells
And pretty maids all in a row.

One, two, buckle my shoe

One, two........................Buckle my shoe.
Three, four.....................Knock at the door.
Five, six........................Pick up sticks.
Seven, eight...................Lay them straight.
Nine, ten.......................A big, fat hen.
Eleven, twelve................Dig and delve.
Thirteen, fourteen..........Maids a-courting.
Fifteen, sixteen..............Maids in the kitchen.
Seventeen, eighteen.......Maids a-waiting.
Nineteen, twenty...........My plate's empty.

Little Jack Horner

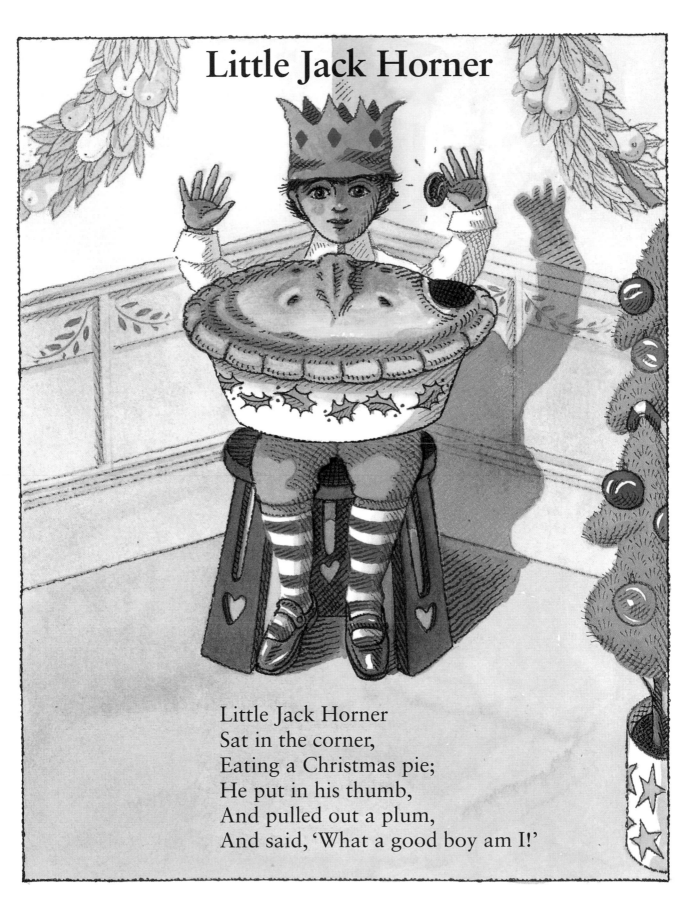

Little Jack Horner
Sat in the corner,
Eating a Christmas pie;
He put in his thumb,
And pulled out a plum,
And said, 'What a good boy am I!'

Hot cross buns

Hot cross buns! Hot cross buns!
One a penny,
Two a penny,
Hot cross buns.

If you have no daughters,
Give them to your sons.

One a penny,
Two a penny,
Hot cross buns.

Jack Sprat

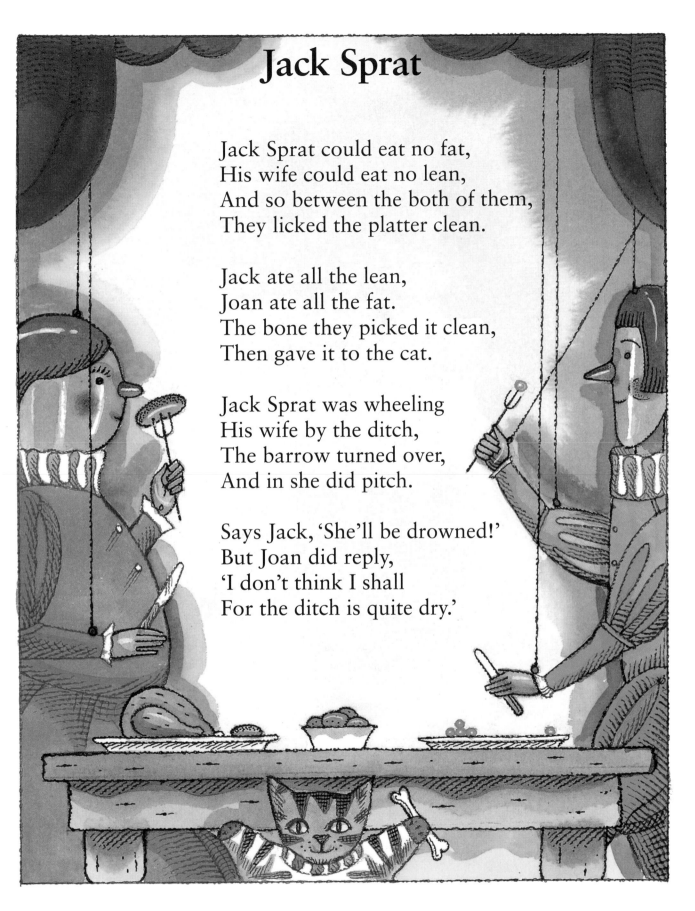

Jack Sprat could eat no fat,
His wife could eat no lean,
And so between the both of them,
They licked the platter clean.

Jack ate all the lean,
Joan ate all the fat.
The bone they picked it clean,
Then gave it to the cat.

Jack Sprat was wheeling
His wife by the ditch,
The barrow turned over,
And in she did pitch.

Says Jack, 'She'll be drowned!'
But Joan did reply,
'I don't think I shall
For the ditch is quite dry.'

Old Mother Hubbard

Old Mother Hubbard
Went to the cupboard
To get her poor dog a bone,
But when she got there
The cupboard was bare
And so the poor dog had none.

She went to the baker's
To buy him some bread,
But when she came back
The poor dog was dead.

She went to the joiner's
To buy him a coffin,
But when she came back
The poor dog was laughing.

She went to the fish-man's
To buy him some fish,
But when she came back
He was licking the dish.

She went to the barber's
To buy him a wig,
But when she came back
He was dancing a jig.

She went to the tailor's
To buy him a coat,
But when she came back
He was riding a goat.

She went to the cobbler's
To buy him some shoes,
But when she came back
He was reading the news.

The dame made a curtsey,
The dog made a bow;
The dame said, 'Your servant.'
The dog said, 'Bow wow.'

Three blind mice

Three blind mice! Three blind mice!
See how they run! See how they run!
They all ran after the farmer's wife,
She cut off their tails with a carving knife,
Did you ever see such a sight in your life
As three blind mice?

Simple Simon

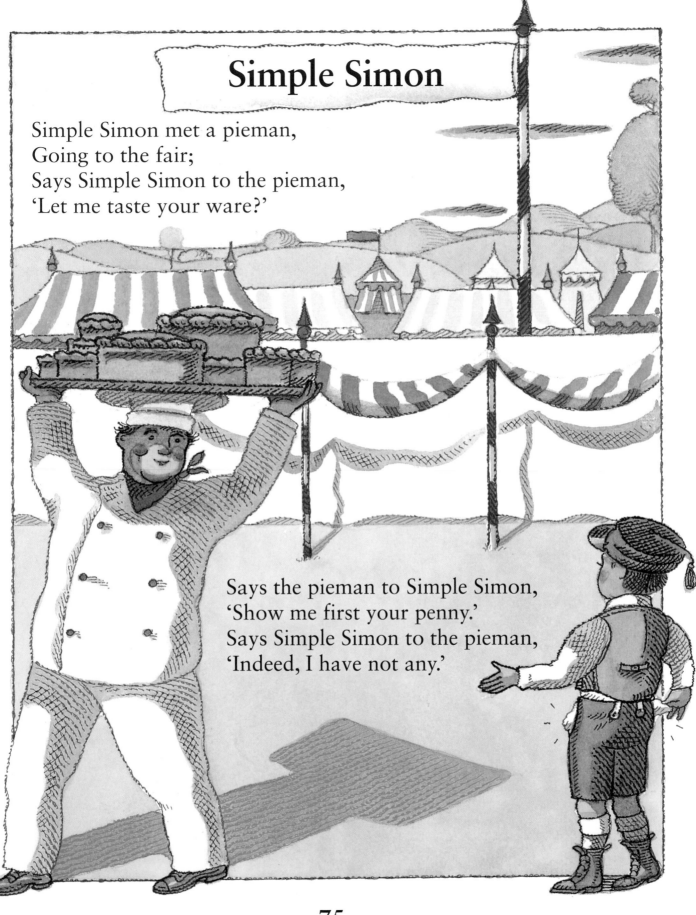

Simple Simon met a pieman,
Going to the fair;
Says Simple Simon to the pieman,
'Let me taste your ware?'

Says the pieman to Simple Simon,
'Show me first your penny.'
Says Simple Simon to the pieman,
'Indeed, I have not any.'

Curly Locks, Curly Locks

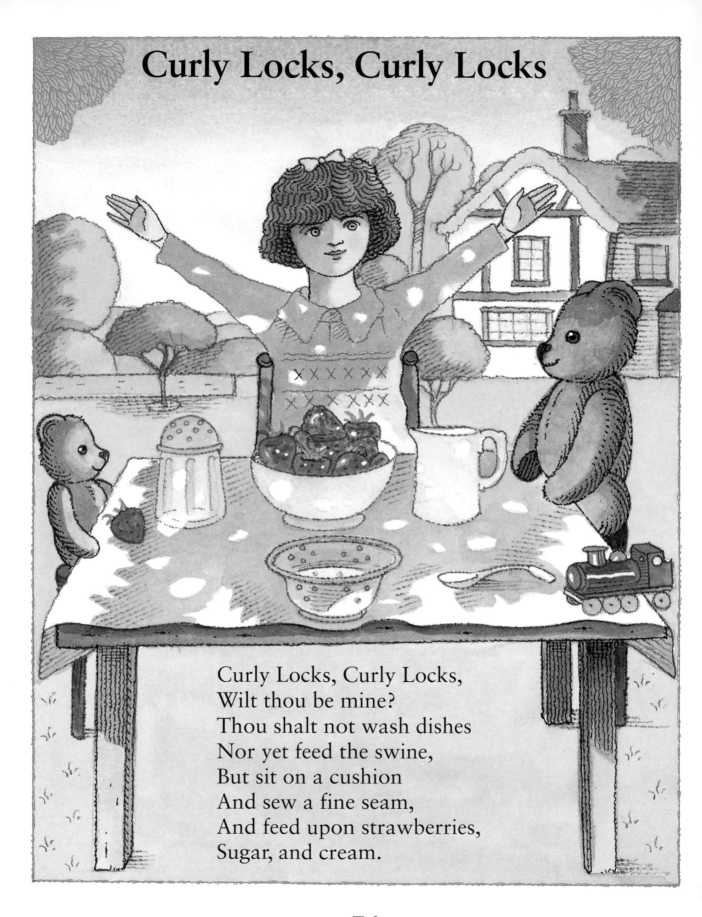

Curly Locks, Curly Locks,
Wilt thou be mine?
Thou shalt not wash dishes
Nor yet feed the swine,
But sit on a cushion
And sew a fine seam,
And feed upon strawberries,
Sugar, and cream.

One, two, three, four, five

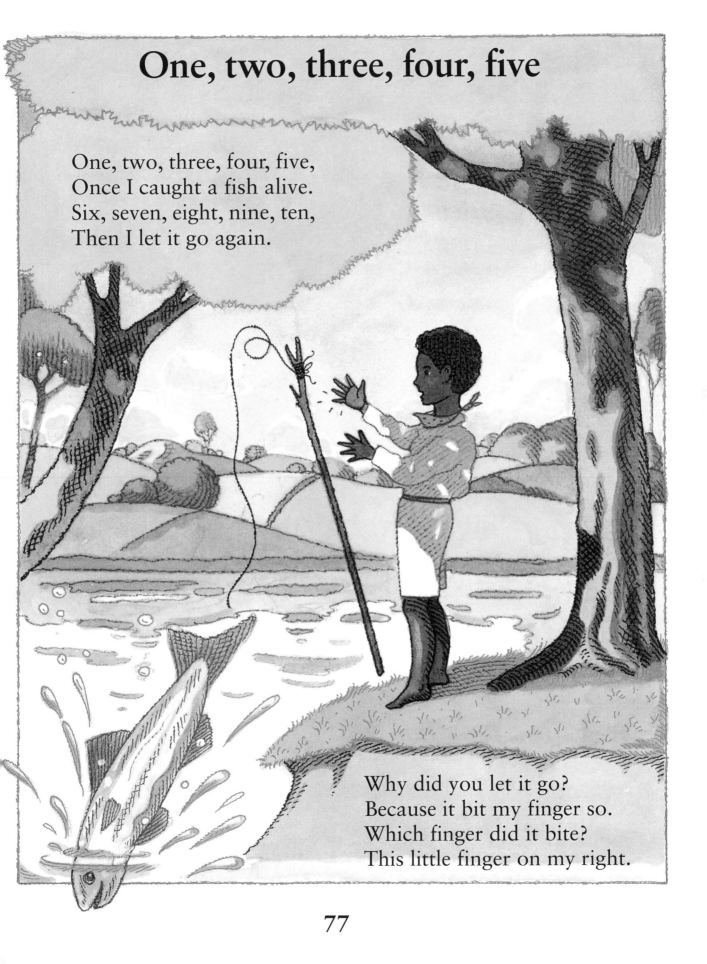

One, two, three, four, five,
Once I caught a fish alive.
Six, seven, eight, nine, ten,
Then I let it go again.

Why did you let it go?
Because it bit my finger so.
Which finger did it bite?
This little finger on my right.

Ding, dong, bell

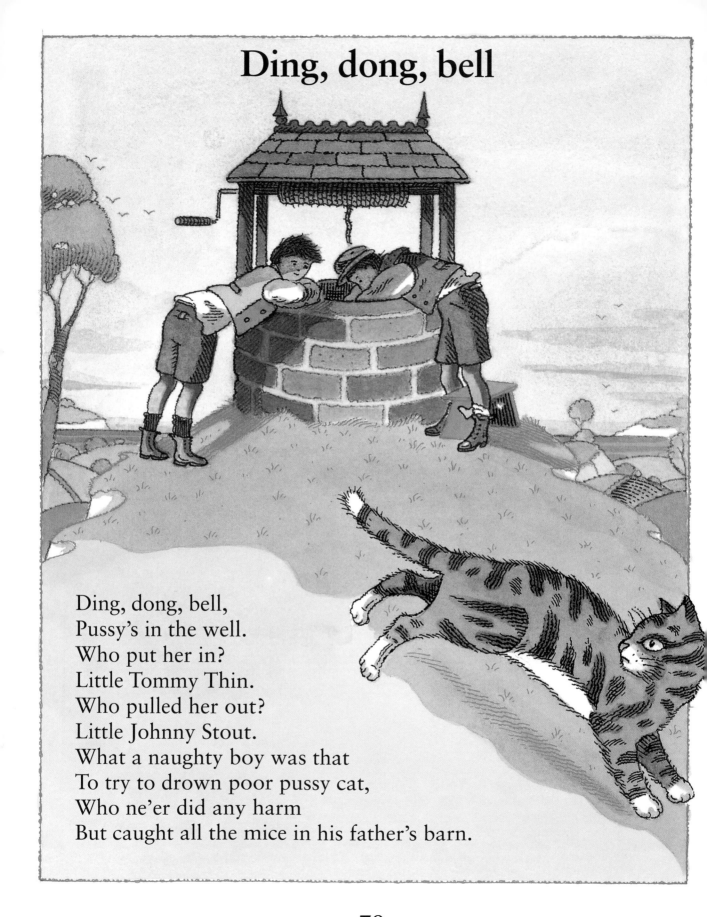

Ding, dong, bell,
Pussy's in the well.
Who put her in?
Little Tommy Thin.
Who pulled her out?
Little Johnny Stout.
What a naughty boy was that
To try to drown poor pussy cat,
Who ne'er did any harm
But caught all the mice in his father's barn.

Jack and Jill

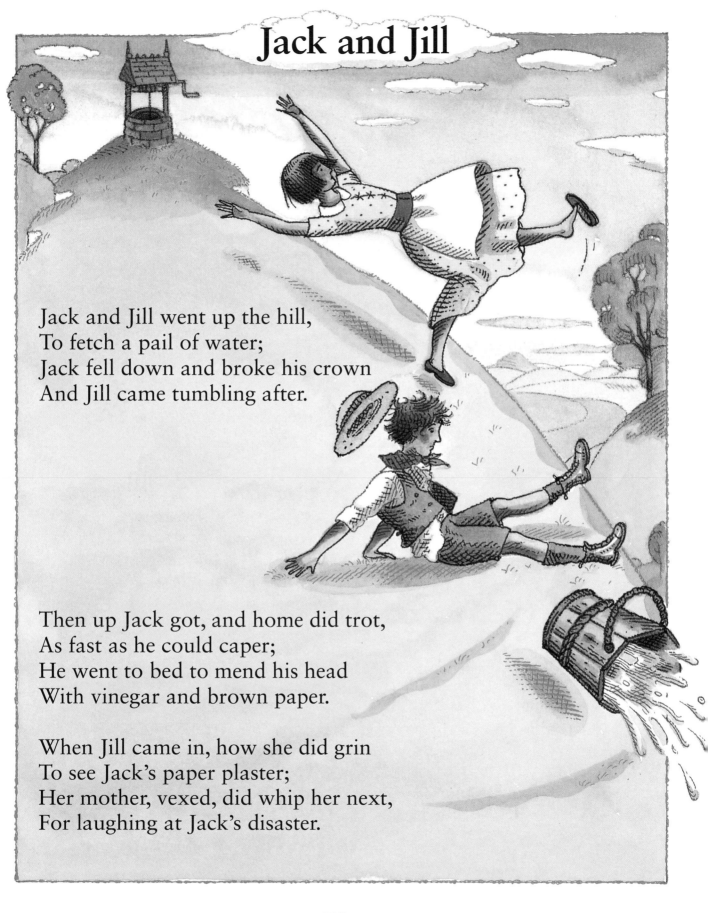

Jack and Jill went up the hill,
To fetch a pail of water;
Jack fell down and broke his crown
And Jill came tumbling after.

Then up Jack got, and home did trot,
As fast as he could caper;
He went to bed to mend his head
With vinegar and brown paper.

When Jill came in, how she did grin
To see Jack's paper plaster;
Her mother, vexed, did whip her next,
For laughing at Jack's disaster.

Little Bo-Peep

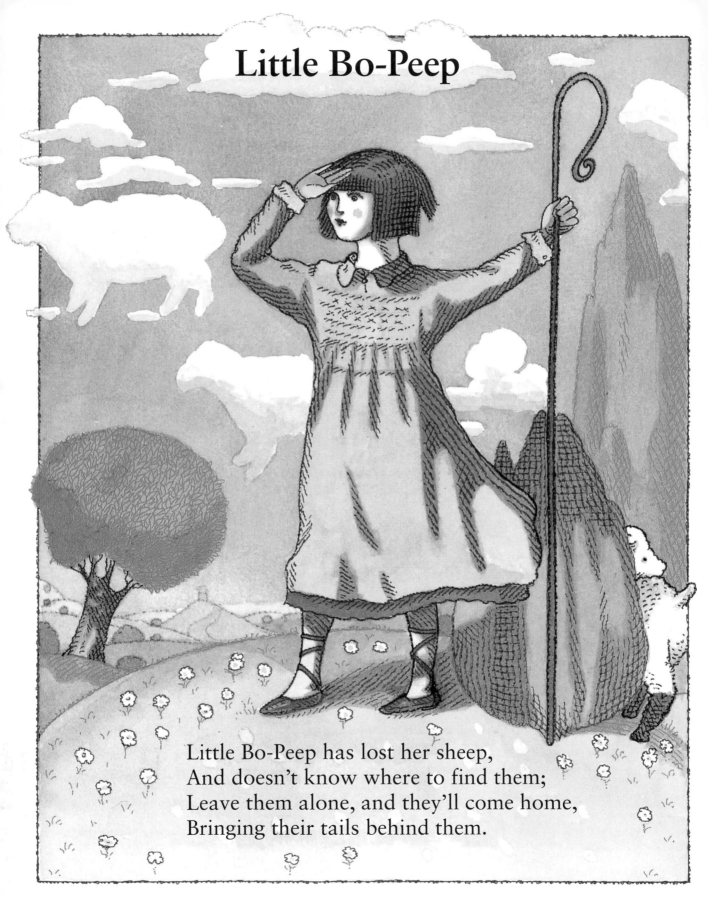

Little Bo-Peep has lost her sheep,
And doesn't know where to find them;
Leave them alone, and they'll come home,
Bringing their tails behind them.

Little boy blue

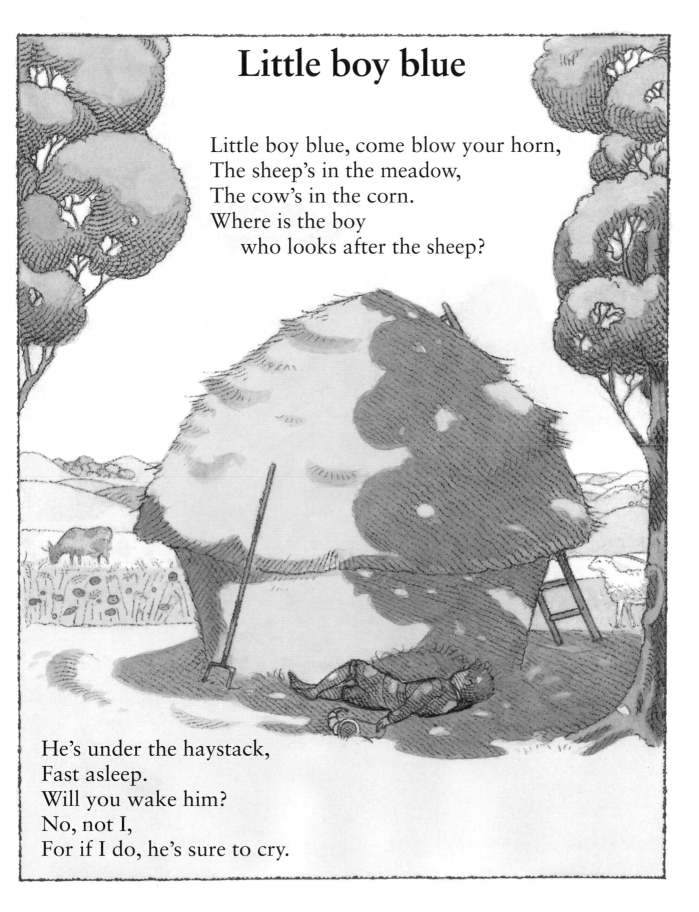

Little boy blue, come blow your horn,
The sheep's in the meadow,
The cow's in the corn.
Where is the boy
who looks after the sheep?

He's under the haystack,
Fast asleep.
Will you wake him?
No, not I,
For if I do, he's sure to cry.

Tom, Tom, the piper's son

Tom, Tom, the piper's son,
Stole a pig, and away did run,
The pig was eat and Tom was beat,
And Tom went crying down the street.

Tom, Tom, the piper's son,
He learned to play when he was young;
But all the tune that he could play
Was 'Over the hills and far away.'

There was a crooked man

There was a crooked man,
And he walked a crooked mile;
He found a crooked sixpence
Against a crooked stile;
He bought a crooked cat,
Who caught a crooked mouse,
And they all lived together
In a little crooked house.

There was an old woman

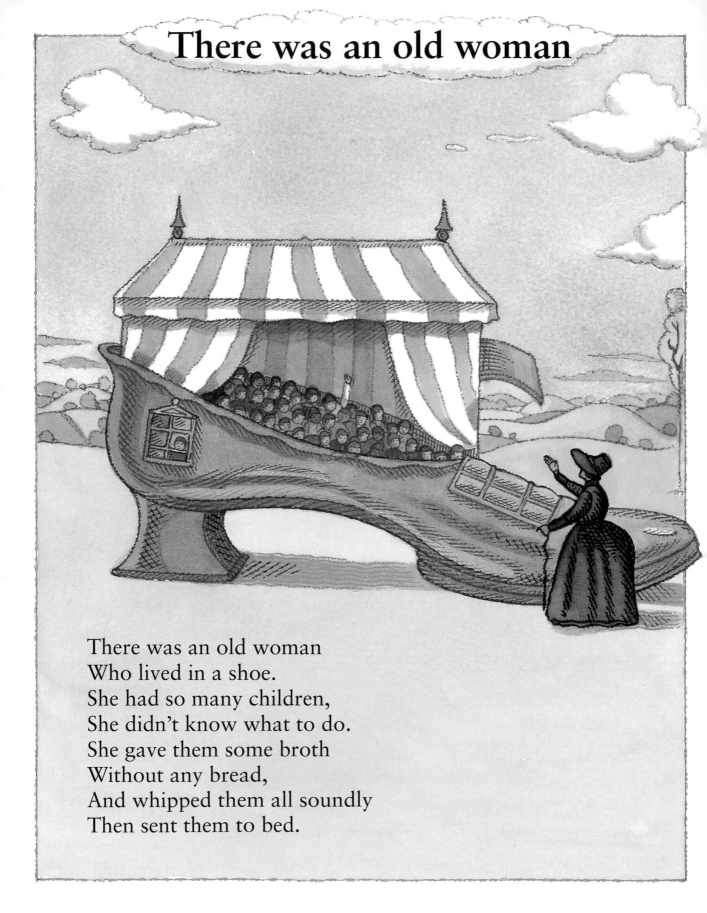

There was an old woman
Who lived in a shoe.
She had so many children,
She didn't know what to do.
She gave them some broth
Without any bread,
And whipped them all soundly
Then sent them to bed.

As I was going to St Ives

As I was going to St Ives,
I met a man with seven wives;
Each wife had seven sacks,
Each sack had seven cats,
Each cat had seven kits:
Kits, cats, sacks, and wives,
How many were there going to St Ives?

Ladybird, ladybird

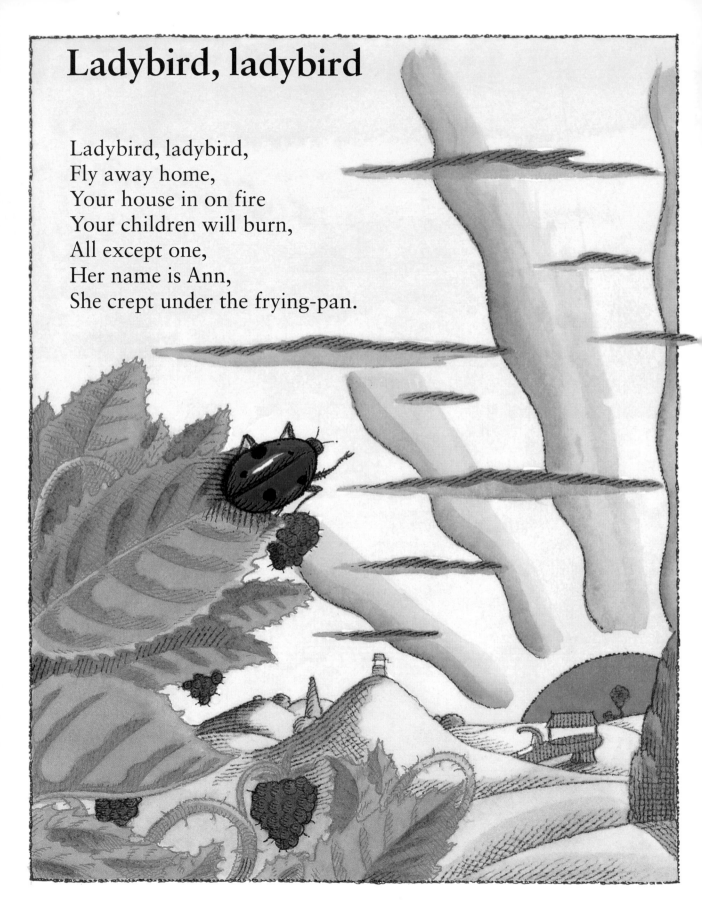

Ladybird, ladybird,
Fly away home,
Your house in on fire
Your children will burn,
All except one,
Her name is Ann,
She crept under the frying-pan.

The north wind doth blow

The north wind doth blow
And we shall have snow,
And what will poor robin do then?
Poor thing!

He'll sit in a barn,
And keep himself warm,
And hide his head under his wing,
Poor thing!

Little Tommy Tucker

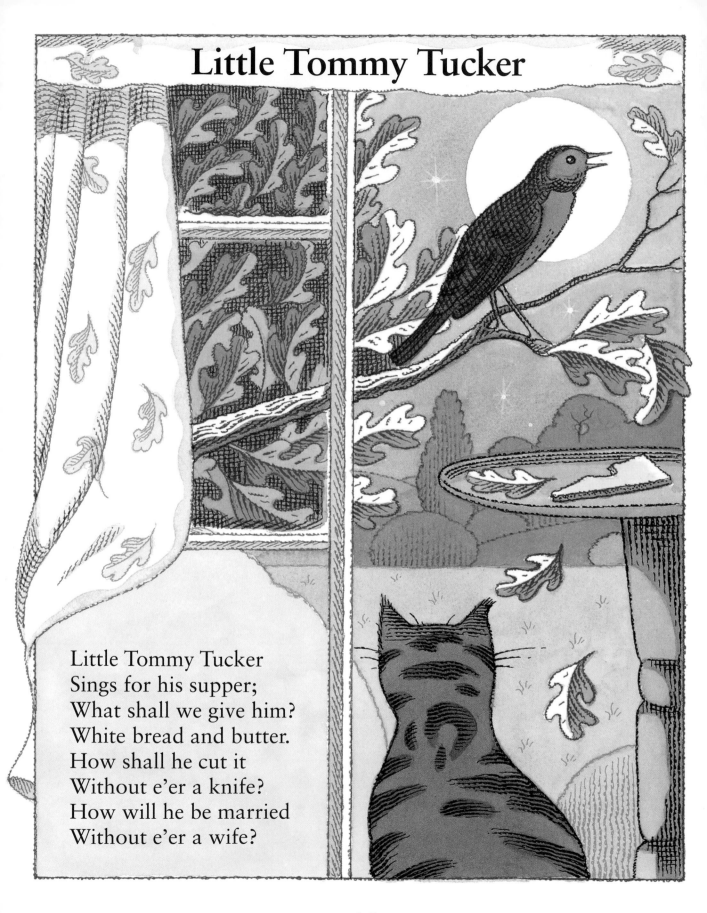

Little Tommy Tucker
Sings for his supper;
What shall we give him?
White bread and butter.
How shall he cut it
Without e'er a knife?
How will he be married
Without e'er a wife?

Goosey, goosey, gander

Goosey, goosey, gander,
Whither shall I wander?
Upstairs and downstairs,
And in my lady's chamber.

There I met an old man
Who wouldn't say his prayers,
I took him by his left leg,
And threw him down the stairs.

Wee Willie Winkie

Wee Willie Winkie,
Runs through the town,
Upstairs and downstairs,
In his nightgown.
Rapping at the window,
Crying through the lock,
Are the children in their beds
For it's now eight o'clock?

Hey! Willie Winkie,
Are you coming then?
The cat's singing pussie,
To the sleeping hen;
The dog's lying on the floor
And does not even peep;
But here's a wakeful laddie,
That will not fall asleep.

Wearied is the mother
That has a restless wean,
A wee, stumpy bairnie
Heard whene'er he's seen;
That has a battle aye with sleep
Before he'll close an e'e,
But a kiss from off his rosy lips
Gives strength anew to me.

The man in the moon

The man in the moon
Came down too soon,
And asked his way to Norwich;
He went by the south,
And burnt his mouth
With supping cold plum porridge.

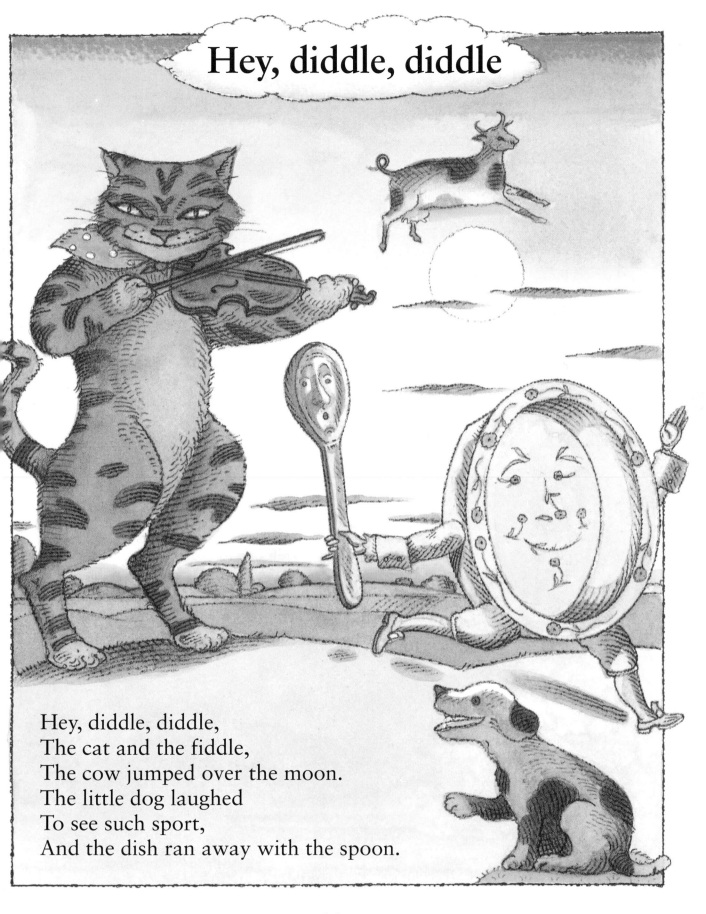

Hey, diddle, diddle

Hey, diddle, diddle,
The cat and the fiddle,
The cow jumped over the moon.
The little dog laughed
To see such sport,
And the dish ran away with the spoon.

Ride a cock-horse

Ride a cock-horse to Banbury Cross,
To see a fine lady upon a white horse;
With rings on her fingers and bells on her toes,
She shall have music wherever she goes.

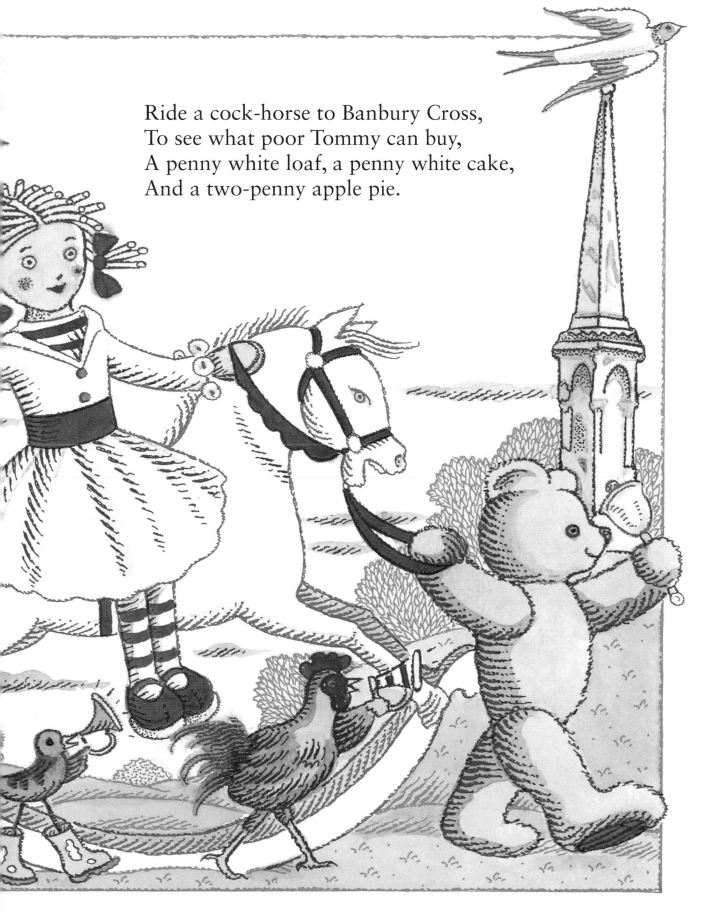

Ride a cock-horse to Banbury Cross,
To see what poor Tommy can buy,
A penny white loaf, a penny white cake,
And a two-penny apple pie.

Ride away

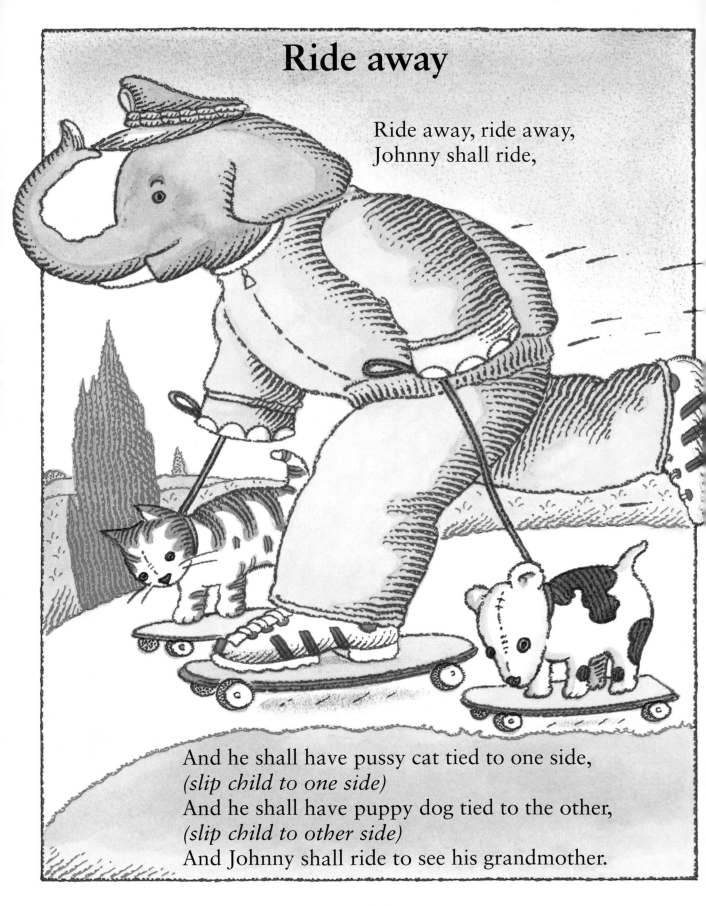

Ride away, ride away,
Johnny shall ride,

And he shall have pussy cat tied to one side,
(slip child to one side)
And he shall have puppy dog tied to the other,
(slip child to other side)
And Johnny shall ride to see his grandmother.

Here comes a lady

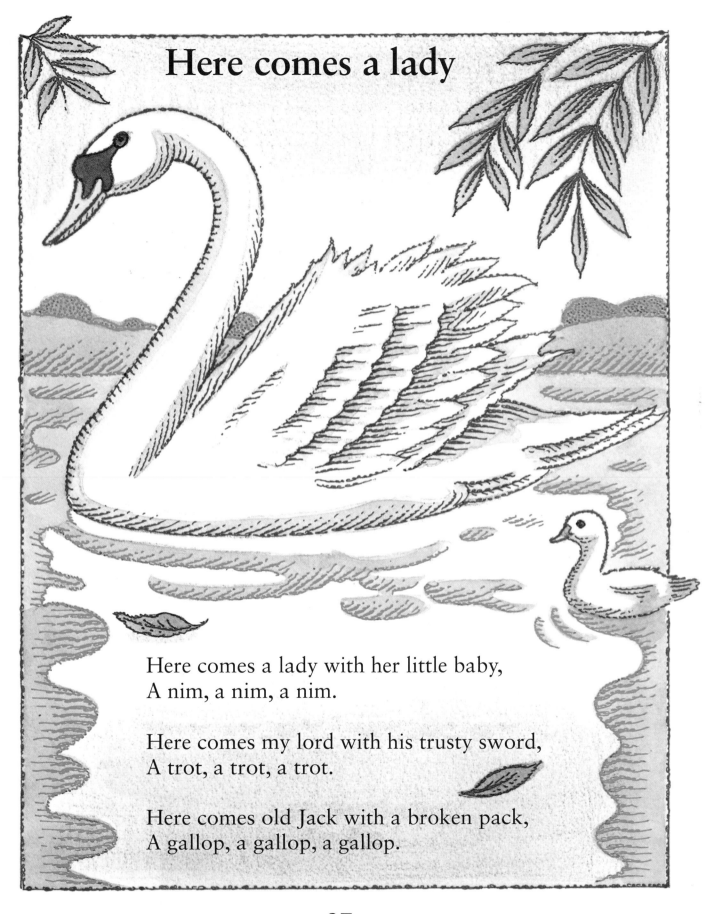

Here comes a lady with her little baby,
A nim, a nim, a nim.

Here comes my lord with his trusty sword,
A trot, a trot, a trot.

Here comes old Jack with a broken pack,
A gallop, a gallop, a gallop.

A farmer went trotting

A farmer went trotting
Upon his grey mare,
Bumpety, bumpety, bump!
With his daughter behind him
So rosy and fair,
Lumpety, lumpety, lump!

A raven cried, 'Croak!'
And they all tumbled DOWN,
(slip child down between knees)
Bumpety, bumpety, bump!
The mare broke her knees,
And the farmer his crown,
Lumpety, lumpety, lump!

The mischievous raven
Flew laughing away,
Bumpety, bumpety, bump!
And he vowed he would serve them
The same the next day,
Lumpety, lumpety, lump!

This is the way the ladies ride

This is the way the ladies ride,
Trippetty tee!
Trippetty tee!
This is the way the ladies ride,
Trippetty, trippetty tee!

This is the way the gentlemen ride,
Gallopy-gallop!
Gallopy-gallop!
This is the way the gentlemen ride,
Gallopy-gallopy-gallop!

This is the way the farmers ride,
Hobbledy-hoy!
Hobbledy-hoy!
This is the way the farmers ride,
Hobbledy-hoy!
Hobbledy-hoy!
And D-O-W-N into the ditch.

Father and Mother, and Uncle John

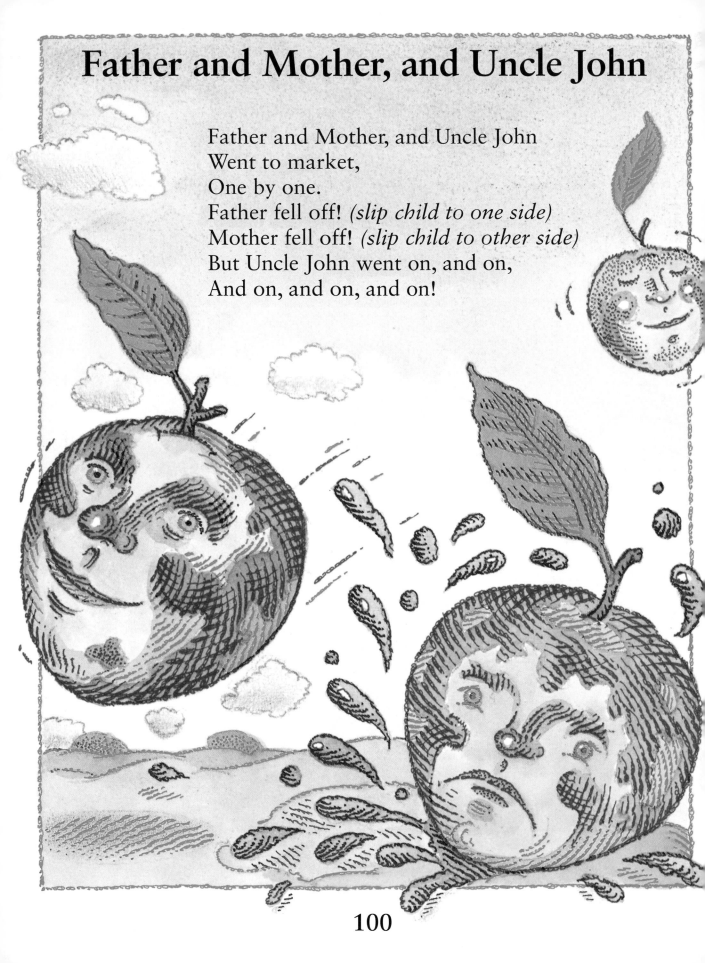

Father and Mother, and Uncle John
Went to market,
One by one.
Father fell off! *(slip child to one side)*
Mother fell off! *(slip child to other side)*
But Uncle John went on, and on,
And on, and on, and on!

To market, to market

To market, to market,
To buy a fat pig;
Home again, home again,
Jiggety-jig.

To market, to market,
To buy a fat hog:
Home again, home again,
Jiggety-jog.

To market, to market,
To buy a plum bun:
Home again, home again,
Market is done.

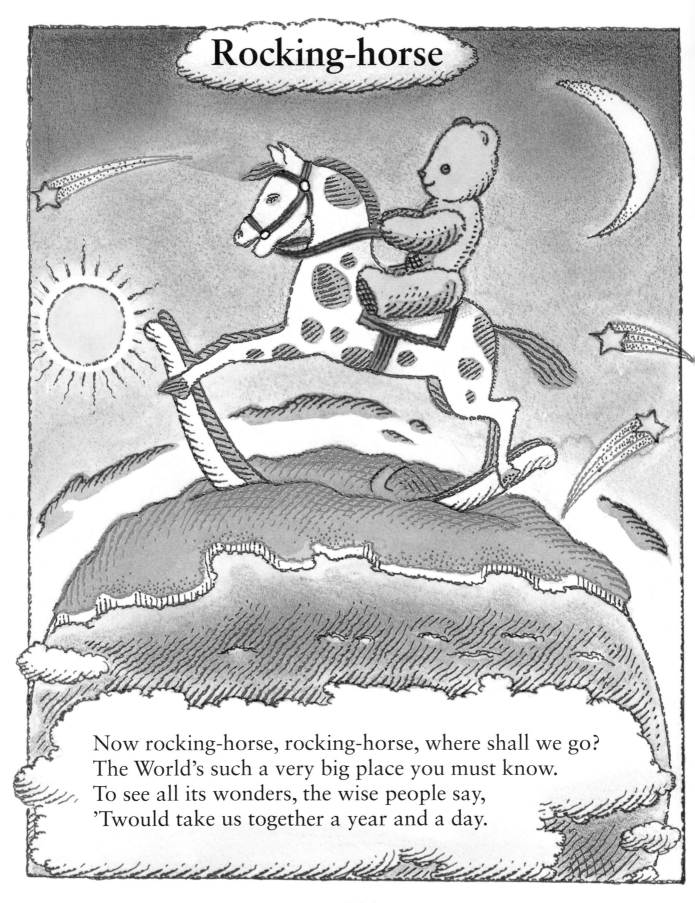

Rocking-horse

Now rocking-horse, rocking-horse, where shall we go?
The World's such a very big place you must know.
To see all its wonders, the wise people say,
'Twould take us together a year and a day.

Trot, trot, trot

Trot, trot, trot,
Go and never stop.
Trudge along, my little pony,
Where 'tis rough and where 'tis stony.
Go and never stop,
Trot, trot, trot, trot, TROT!

Dance, little baby

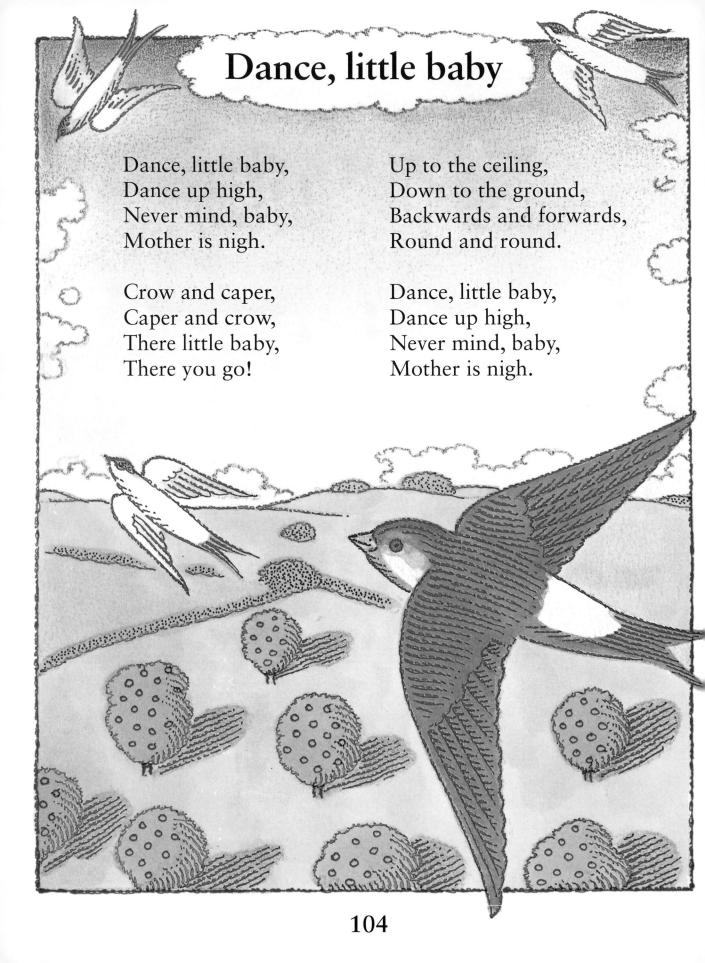

Dance, little baby,
Dance up high,
Never mind, baby,
Mother is nigh.

Crow and caper,
Caper and crow,
There little baby,
There you go!

Up to the ceiling,
Down to the ground,
Backwards and forwards,
Round and round.

Dance, little baby,
Dance up high,
Never mind, baby,
Mother is nigh.

Katie Beardie

Katie Beardie had a cow,
Black and white about the mou,
Wasn'a that a dainty cow?
  Dance, Katie Beardie!

Katie Beardie had a hen,
Cackled but and cackled ben,
Wasn'a that a dainty hen?
  Dance, Katie Beardie!

Katie Beardie had a cock,
That could spin, and bake, and rock,
Wasn'a that a dainty cock?
  Dance, Katie Beardie!

Katie Beardie had a grice,
It could skate upon the ice;
Wasn'a that a dainty grice?
  Dance, Katie Beardie!

Dance to your daddy

Dance to your daddy,
My bonnie laddy,
Dance to your daddy,
My bonnie lamb.

You shall get a fishy,
In a little dishy,
You shall get a fishy,
When the boat comes in.

You shall get a coatie,
And a pair of breekies,
And you'll get an eggy,
And a bit of ham.

You shall get a pony,
Fit to ride for ony,
And you'll get a whippy,
For to make him gang.

Dance to your daddy,
My bonnie laddy,
Dance to your daddy,
My bonnie lamb.

106

Down at the station

Down at the station,
Early in the morning,
Two little puffer trains,
All in a row.

Man at the engine,
Turns the little handle,
Chuff-chuff-chuff and away we go,
Chuff-chuff-chuff,
Chuff-chuff-chuff,
Chuff-chuff-chuff-CHUFF.

Higgledy-Piggledy

Higgledy-Piggledy,
My black hen,
She lays eggs
    for gentlemen;
Sometimes nine,
And sometimes ten,
Higgledy-Piggledy,
    My black hen!

108

Rub-a-dub-dub

Rub-a-dub-dub
Three men in a tub,
And who do you think were there?
The butcher, the baker,
The candlestick-maker,
All going to the fair.

Cock-crow

The cock's on the house-top
Blowing his horn.
The bull's in the barn,
A-threshing of corn.
The maids in the meadow
Are making the hay.
The ducks in the river
Are swimming away.

Handy-Spandy

Handy-Spandy, jack-a-dandy,
Loved plum cake and sugar candy!
He bought some at a grocer's shop,
And then he goes hop, hop, a-hop!

Barber, barber

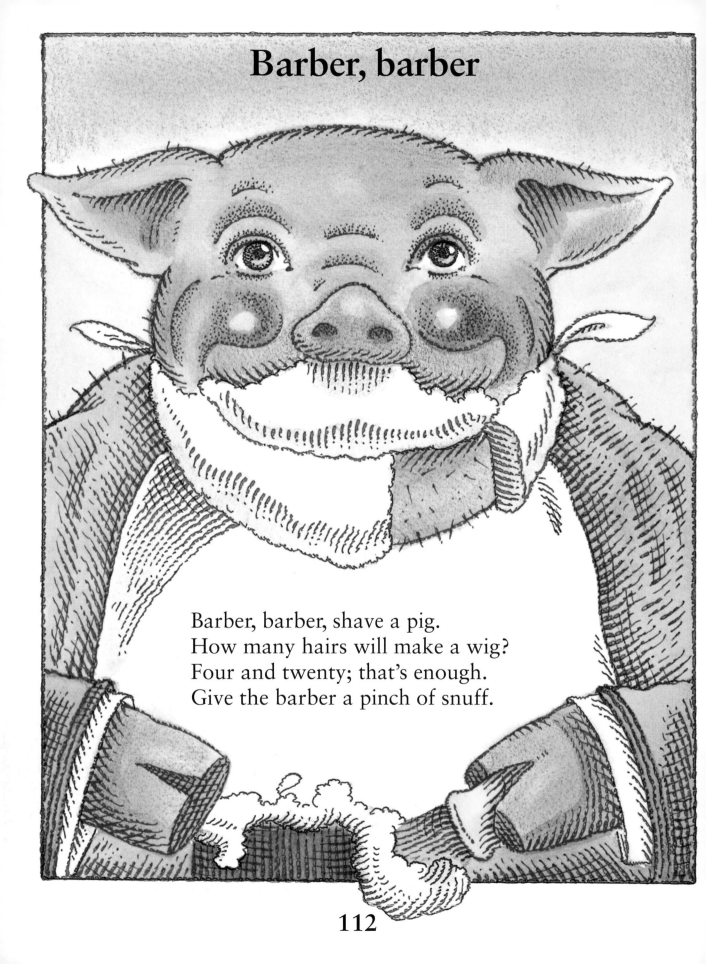

Barber, barber, shave a pig.
How many hairs will make a wig?
Four and twenty; that's enough.
Give the barber a pinch of snuff.

Clap, clap handies

Clap, clap handies,
Mummy's wee bairn,
Clap, clap handies.
Daddy's coming home,
Home to his bonnie wee lassie,
Clap, clap handies.

Diddle, diddle dumpling

Diddle, diddle, dumpling,
My son John
Went to bed with his trousers on;
One shoe off and one shoe on,
Diddle, diddle, dumpling,
My son John.

Doggie's way

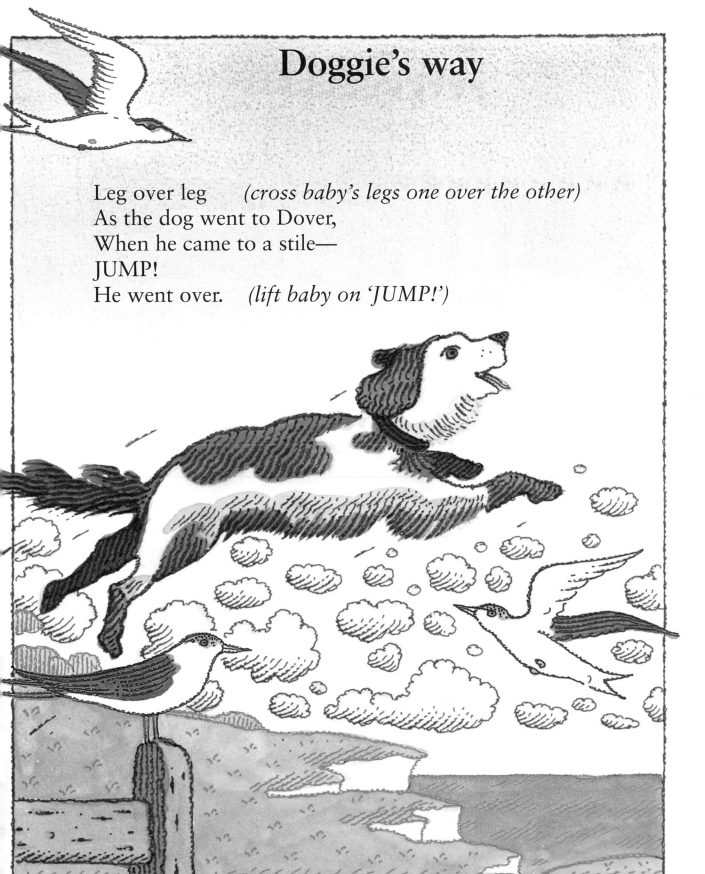

Leg over leg   *(cross baby's legs one over the other)*
As the dog went to Dover,
When he came to a stile—
JUMP!
He went over.   *(lift baby on 'JUMP!')*

Up to the heavens

Up to the heavens,
Down to the sea,
How many fishes can you see?
One—two—three—four—FIVE.

See-saw Sacradown

See-saw Sacradown,
Which is the way
To London Town?
One foot up,
The other foot down,
That is the way
To London Town.

The little duck

I think it was the best of luck,
That I was born a little duck,
With yellow feet and yellow shoes,
Just fit to waddle where I choose.

Hob, shoe, hob

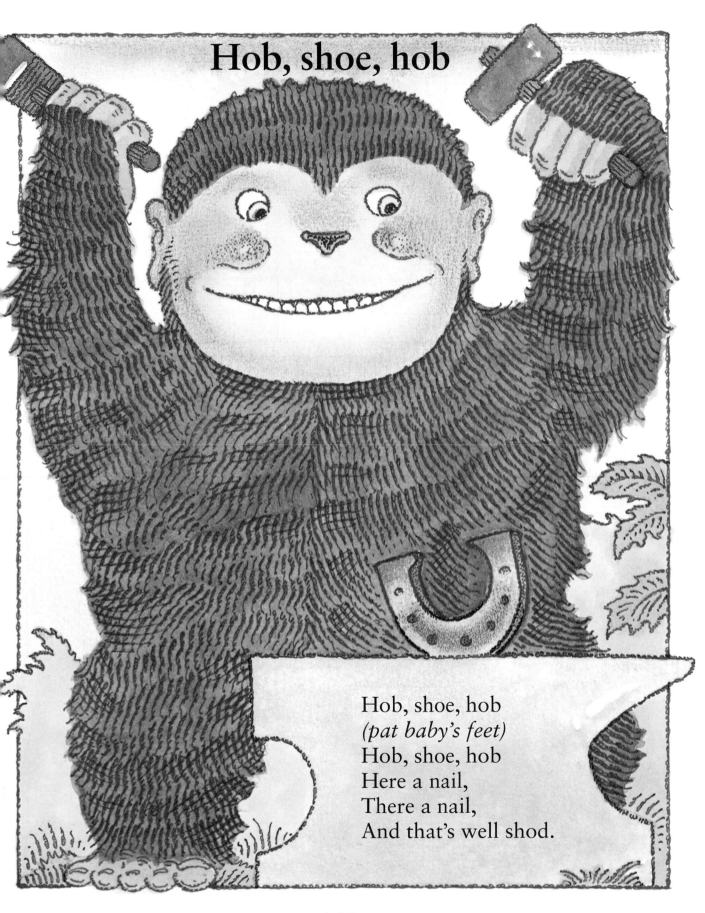

Hob, shoe, hob
(pat baby's feet)
Hob, shoe, hob
Here a nail,
There a nail,
And that's well shod.

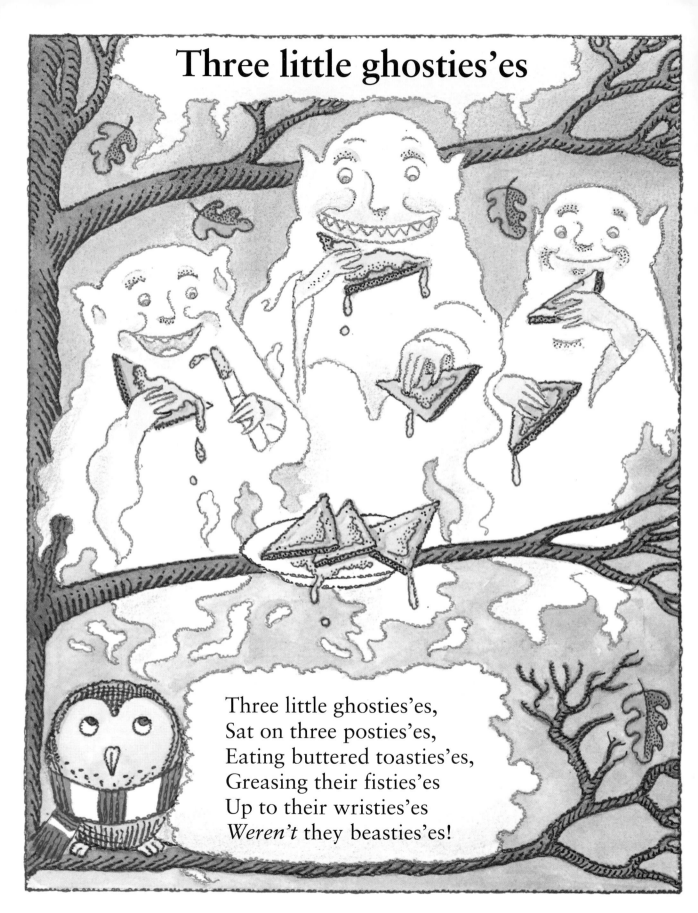

Three little ghosties'es

Three little ghosties'es,
Sat on three posties'es,
Eating buttered toasties'es,
Greasing their fisties'es
Up to their wristies'es
Weren't they beasties'es!

Shoe a little horse

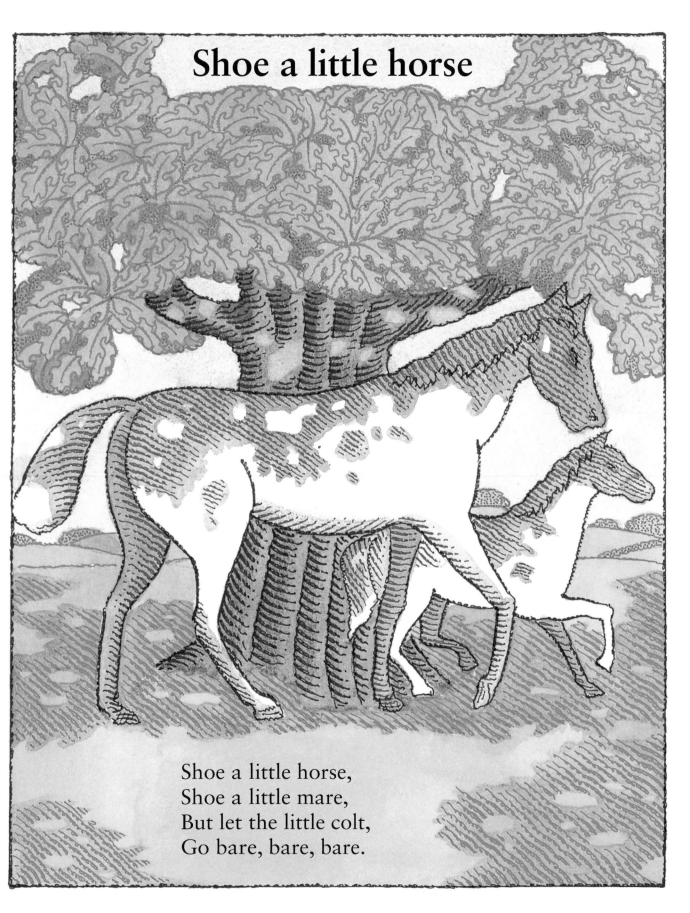

Shoe a little horse,
Shoe a little mare,
But let the little colt,
Go bare, bare, bare.

Bye baby bunting

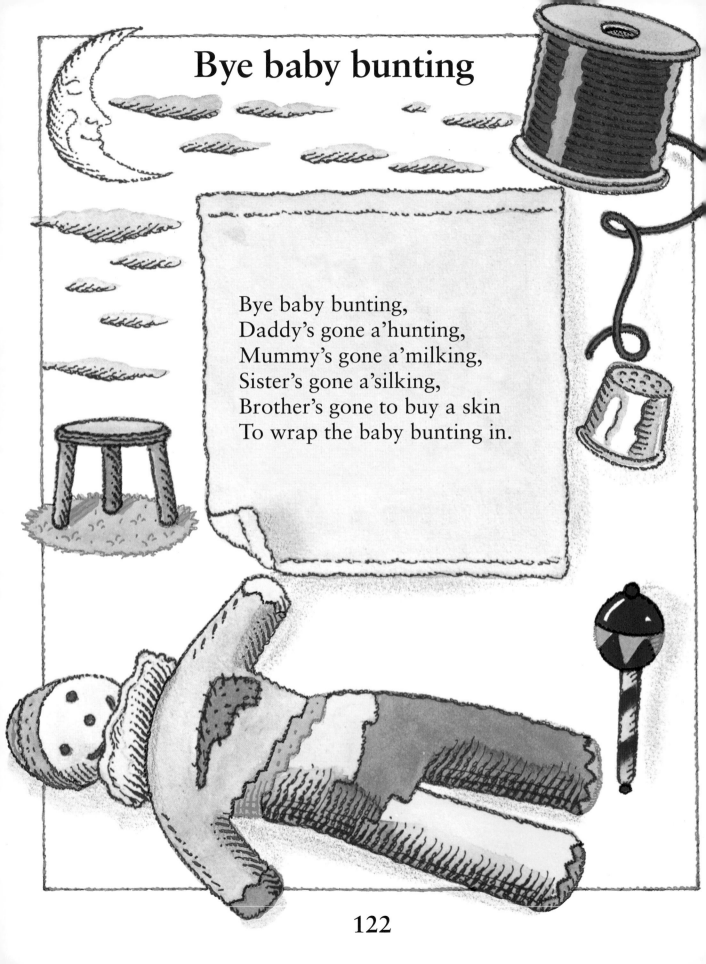

Bye baby bunting,
Daddy's gone a'hunting,
Mummy's gone a'milking,
Sister's gone a'silking,
Brother's gone to buy a skin
To wrap the baby bunting in.

Sleepy song

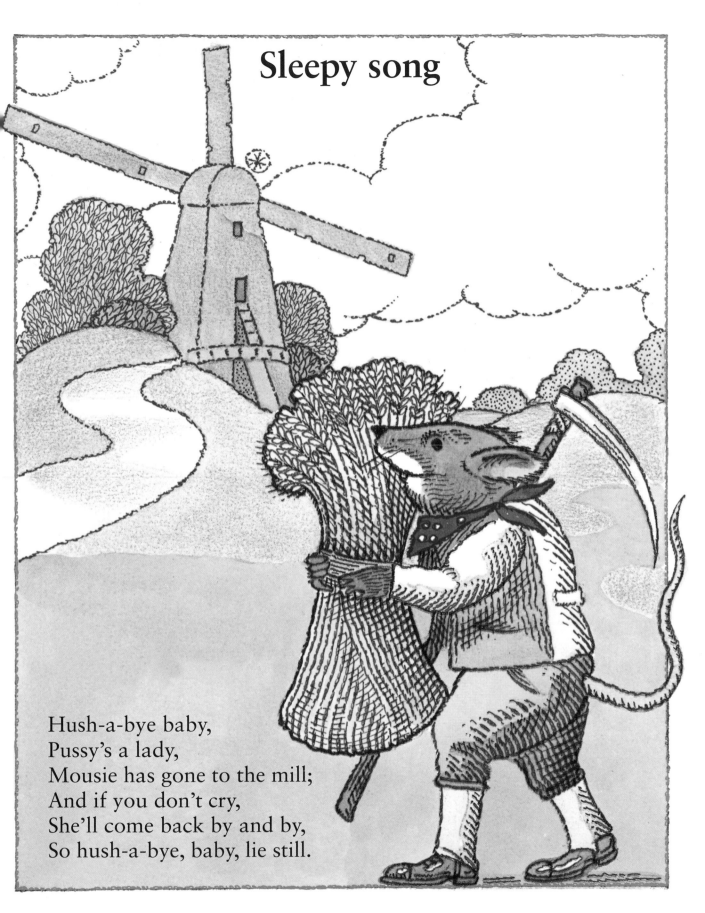

Hush-a-bye baby,
Pussy's a lady,
Mousie has gone to the mill;
And if you don't cry,
She'll come back by and by,
So hush-a-bye, baby, lie still.

Lullaby

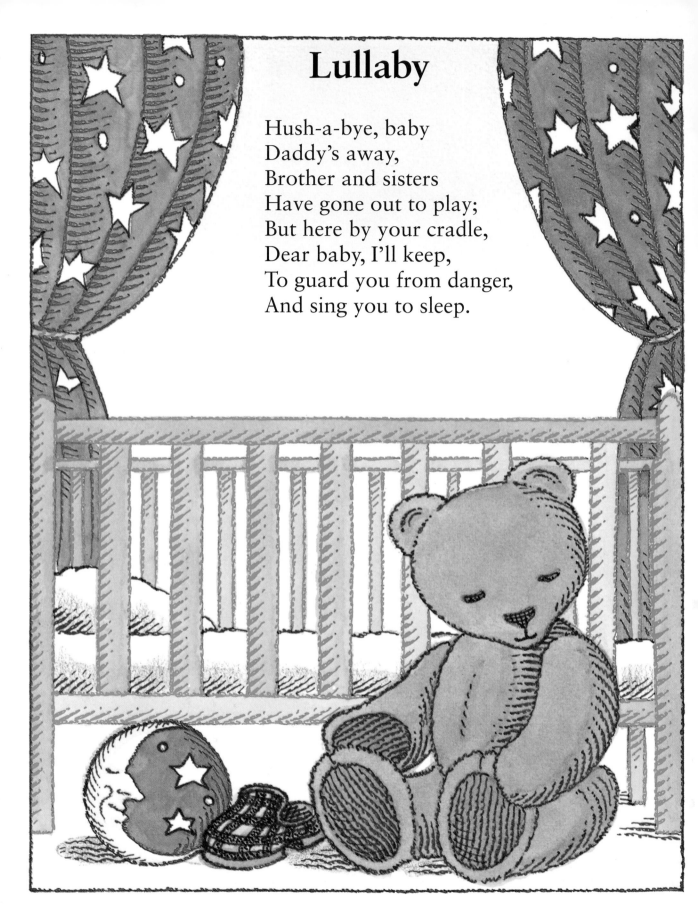

Hush-a-bye, baby
Daddy's away,
Brother and sisters
Have gone out to play;
But here by your cradle,
Dear baby, I'll keep,
To guard you from danger,
And sing you to sleep.

Baby beds

Little lambs, little lambs,
Where do you sleep?
'In the green meadow
With mother sheep.'

Little birds, little birds,
Where do you rest?
'Close to our mother
In a warm nest.'

Baby dear, baby dear,
Where do you lie?
'In my warm bed
With mother close by.'

Evening

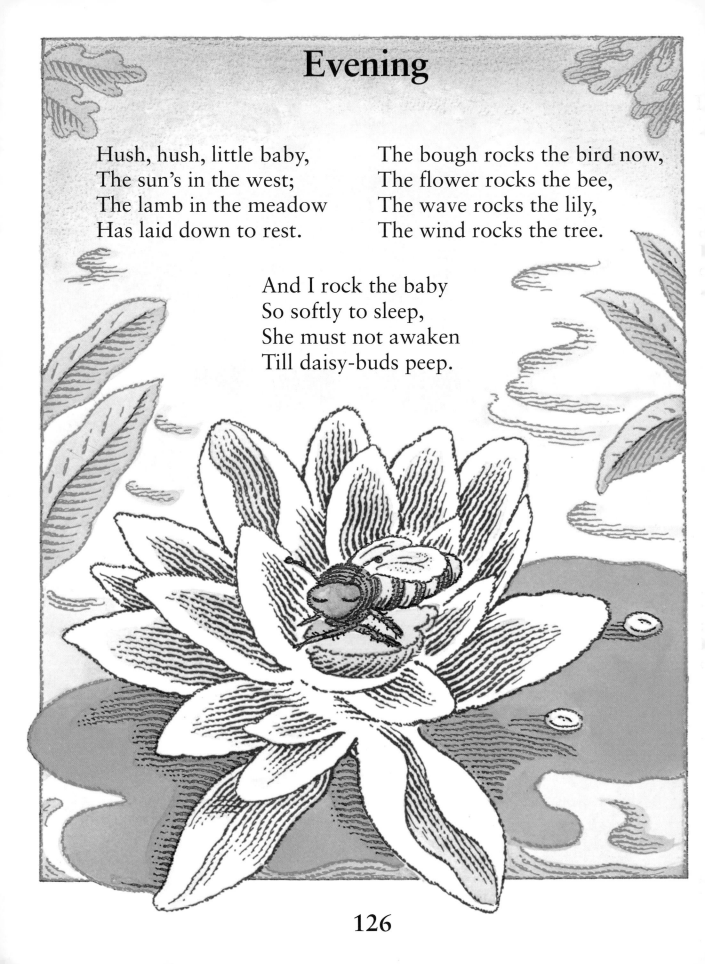

Hush, hush, little baby,
The sun's in the west;
The lamb in the meadow
Has laid down to rest.

The bough rocks the bird now,
The flower rocks the bee,
The wave rocks the lily,
The wind rocks the tree.

And I rock the baby
So softly to sleep,
She must not awaken
Till daisy-buds peep.

Notes for interactive rhymes

The rhymes on **pages 94–126** can all be enjoyed with simple actions. Use these notes to make the most of these rhymes and lullabies.

Knee-jogging rhymes

These are very rhythmic rhymes where the baby rides on your knees or crossed legs. The rate of jogging varies with the rhythm of the words, but usually starts quite gently and ends vigorously. (**Pages 94–103**)

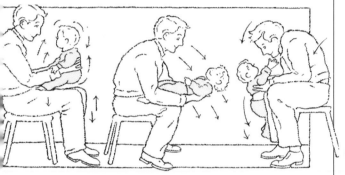

Patting and clapping rhymes

Babies love having their feet patted and their hands clapped. Pat and clap to the rhythm of the words, wiggle legs and tickle as appropriate. (**Pages 113–121**)

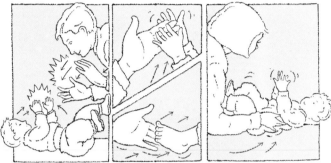

Bouncing and dancing rhymes

These are played by bouncing the baby on your lap or holding it while it 'dances' on your knee. Lifting the baby in the air and bringing it down between your knees is a feature of some of the rhymes. (**Pages 104–112**)

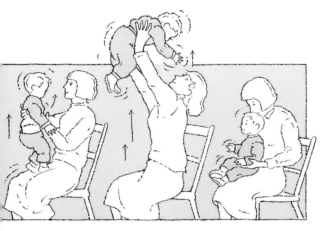

Lullabies and Rocking Rhymes

These are sleeping songs for you and the baby, having a cuddle or gently rocking to and fro or side to side. (**Pages 122–126**)

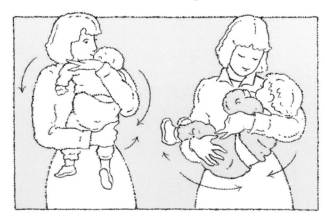

OXFORD
UNIVERSITY PRESS

Great Clarendon Street, Oxford OX2 6DP.
United Kingdom

Oxford University Press is a department of the University of Oxford.
It furthers the University's objective of excellence in research,
scholarship, and education by publishing worldwide

Oxford is a registered trade mark of Oxford University Press
in the UK and in certain other countries

Selection, arrangement, and editorial matter
Copyright © Oxford University Press 1983, 1985, 1986, 1989, 2014
Illustrations copyright © Ian Beck 1983, 1985, 1986, 1989, 2014

The moral rights of the authors/illustrator have been asserted
Database right Oxford University Press (maker)

Previously published as *Round and Round the Garden* (1983), *Oranges and Lemons* (1985),
Ride a Cock Horse (1986), and *Pudding and Pie* (1989)

This edition first published in 2014

All rights reserved. No part of this publication may be reproduced, stored in a retrieval system,
or transmitted, in any form or by any means, without the prior permission in writing of Oxford
University Press, or as expressly permitted by law, by licence or under terms agreed with the
appropriate reprographics rights organization. Enquiries concerning reproduction outside the scope
of the above should be sent to the Rights Department, Oxford University Press, at the address above.

You must not circulate this book in any other binding or cover
and you must impose this same condition on any acquirer

British Library Cataloguing in Publication Data
Data available

ISBN: 978-0-19-273866-0 (paperback)

1 2 3 4 5 6 7 8 9 10

Printed in India

Paper used in the production of this book is a natural,
recyclable product made from wood grown in sustainable forests.
The manufacturing process conforms to the environmental
regulations of the country of origin.

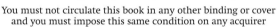